Better Government at Half the Price

Better Government at Half the Price:

Private Production of Public Services

James T. Bennett
Manuel H. Johnson

CAROLINE HOUSE PUBLISHERS, INC.
Ottawa, IL. & Ossining, NY

Copies of this book may be purchased from the publisher for $5.95. All inquiries should be addressed to Caroline House Publishers, Inc., Box 738, Ottawa, Illinois 61350. (815) 434-7905.
ISBN: 0-89803-048-X

Library of Congress Cataloging in Publication Data
Bennett, James T
  Better government at half the price.

  Includes bibliographical references and index.
  1. United States—Appropriations and expenditures—Cost effectiveness. 2. Expenditures, Public—Cost effectiveness. I. Johnson, Manuel H., joint author. II. Title.
HJ7539.B46   353.0072   80-26361
ISBN 0-89803-048-X (pbk.)

CONTENTS

LIST OF TABLES

FOREWORD
by
William E. Simon

Bennett and Johnson's book is a significant contribution to the current debate about the role of government in contemporary American society. In recent years, even a casual observer must be aware of the rapid and dangerous expansion of government at all levels and the increasing intrusion of the public sector into virtually every aspect of social, political, and economic life. Although government has assumed a much greater role in national activities, little progress seems to have been made in solving national problems. On the contrary, government often appears to exacerbate them. Frustration with government has produced an active movement to limit spending, balance budgets, and cut taxes; alternatively, there are persistent calls for more government regulation and controls. However, every taxpayer, regardless of political persuasion, should be vitally concerned about and interested in the theme of this powerful and persuasive book: Public services can be produced with many fewer tax dollars if the more efficient private sector, instead of wasteful and inefficient government agencies, produces these services.

The argument that taxes can be substantially reduced without affecting either the quality or the quantity of public services is carefully developed and tightly reasoned. First, Bennett and Johnson show that the burden on taxpayers has been growing rapidly, is currently at an all-time high, and must increase further in the future to meet financial commitments made by governments in the past. Not only do taxes take more than one-third of the average worker's income, but also the actions of government (regulations and paperwork requirements) raise the prices of goods and services bought by the consumer so that the total burden of government is even greater. Further, it is pointed out that, although government spending at all levels has skyrocketed, many programs have not been effective: there has been a wide gap between government promises and government performance. Taxpayers have been paying more and getting less; it is essential that public services be produced at much lower cost.

Second, the authors explain *why* government has not been and cannot be an efficient producer. The incentive structure in bureaucracy is perverse in that employees cannot be punished for waste and inefficiency, nor rewarded for cost-cutting. Promotion, salary, and prestige in government are obtained by increasing spending, not by reducing spending. If government programs performed properly and solved problems, the existence of agencies would be threatened as well as the jobs of public employees. Thus, there are rewards for failure, but none for success. In contrast, a private sector firm must produce at the lowest possible cost or competition from other firms (both foreign and domestic) will drive it from the market. Efficiency is essential for survival in the private sector because of competition; by law, government agencies are totally insulated from competitive pressures.

Third, numerous case studies of activities performed by the private sector and by local, state, and federal government are compared with regard to cost. In every case, the private sector markedly outperforms the public sector by producing goods and services for the public at much lower cost. So pervasive is the evidence that the Bureaucratic Rule of Two has been proposed: Transfer of a service from the private to the public sector doubles its costs of production.

Fourth, Bennett and Johnson recognize that the practice of contracting out to the private sector has many critics. They meticulously examine the arguments against private production of public services to show that waste, corruption, contract boondoggles, and the like occur because public employees do not protect the interests of the taxpayer. Therefore, the criticism against contracting out should be directed against the public sector, not the private sector.

Finally, federal procurement policy is examined. Although officially the federal government attempts to encourage the private sector as a producer, evidence and case studies are cited that indicate that this policy is not practiced.

This book provides very timely and important insights into the role and functioning of government at all levels. Moreover, it directly addresses a critical public policy issue: the need to reduce the tax burden on American taxpayers without sacrificing necessary public services. The clear and unmistakable conclusion drawn from irrefutable evidence that taxes can be cut substantially without adverse effects on public services should be welcomed by all.

PREFACE

Our interest in the comparison of the costs of production provided by both the public and the private sectors is largely due to accident. One of the authors moved to a new home a short distance from his old residence and still within the same political jurisdiction. Refuse collection was provided by local government in one location, but by the private sector in the other. When the change was made from public to private service, the price paid for trash collection was cut in half and the frequency of collection doubled. As economists who had never given much thought to such matters, the fact that private firms were willing to provide twice the service at half the price charged by local government came as a surprise. After all, public agencies do not operate to earn profits, do not pay taxes of any kind, and are often subsidized by tax dollars in addition to fees received for service. The public firm should, therefore, provide service at far lower costs than "greedy" profit-seeking firms.

Our curiosity was piqued. Was this an isolated incident of bureaucratic inefficiency or was there other evidence that private firms were far superior to the public sector? A search of the economic literature revealed numerous studies that confirmed the latter. The evidence was overwhelming, because, to our knowledge, there is not one case which has been reported that finds the public sector more efficient than the private sector.

The conclusion that the private sector can produce services at lower cost than the public sector raises some very important issues. Why is government inherently inefficient? For years, the orthodoxy of economics and other disciplines has been that government serves the "public interest." Yet, how can this be the case if the taxpayer pays more to a public agency (which should have an enormous cost advantage to begin with, as mentioned above) for a service than would be paid to a "greedy" private firm? Are waste and inefficiency integral characteristics of government? The answers to these questions, provided in Chapter 3, are based upon the insightful and stimulating work of Paul Craig Roberts. Roberts has long argued that government employees are no different from employees in private firms: both respond to incentives in their respective economic environments to maximize their own self-interest. In the public sector, employees are not punished for being wasteful, but are in fact often *rewarded* for inefficiency. In the private sector, waste cannot be tolerated, because competition will eliminate inefficiency. If we have made a contribution to the understanding of this simple, yet powerful, idea, it is because we have built upon the concepts developed and articulated by Roberts.

Our comprehension of bureaucratic organizations has also been greatly advanced by the work of Professor Gordon Tullock at the Public Choice Center of Virginia Polytechnic Institute and State University. On many occasions (and with grace and good humor), he has encouraged our efforts, corrected our errors, and provided invaluable guidance. Others have made contributions to this book. We gratefully acknowledge the helpful suggestions made by Hal Gordon, William Dennis, and Jean Caffiaux. Peter Germanis provided outstanding research assistance. Remaining errors of commission or omission are, of course, entirely our own.

Finally, we wish to express our thanks to Jeff MacNelly, whose cartoons appear throughout the book and capture perfectly the essence of our arguments.

1

INTRODUCTION

The average American, unless living in a world of fantasy and delusion, must be frantic about his or her economic prospects for the future. While inflation is eroding the purchasing power of our earnings, taxes at the federal, state, and local levels of government are soaring. The inevitable result is that living standards are declining: more and more of us cannot afford to buy homes and cars and are finding it increasingly difficult just to make ends meet. Inflation, as both professional economists and laymen widely recognize, is fueled by government deficit spending. Yet we are told that elimination of the deficit would require increasing taxes or cutting essential government services. There is, it seems, no reasonable alternative. As a result, most Americans are frustrated and becoming distrustful of both government and the economic system of private enterprise.

We propose a simple and workable alternative to the problems caused by higher taxes and government deficits. We will show that taxes can be cut drastically at the federal, state, and local levels of government without any reduction in the quality or quantity of public services. The taxpayer can "have his cake and eat it too" because it is possible to get many more goods and services for far fewer tax dollars if the goods and services are produced more efficiently—that is, at lower cost. This can be achieved by having goods and services produced by private enterprise rather than by government. The evidence proving that this can be done (and in fact already has been done) is both overwhelming and irrefutable.

We have compared a wide range of activities carried on by private firms and by state, local, or federal government with respect to cost. Whether you consider airline services, ship repair, debt collection, health services, electric power generation, fire protection, trash collection, or a number of other services, the findings are always the same: the private sector can produce the same or a better quality and quantity of goods and services at a much lower cost than can the public sector. The evidence is so overwhelming that the Bureaucratic Rule of Two has been proposed: "Transfer of a service from private to public hands doubles the cost of production!" To our knowledge, no one has ever shown a single instance in which the public sector has outperformed (or even equaled) the private by producing goods and services at lower (or equivalent) costs.

The nation's taxpayers can no longer afford the luxury of government that drains our pocketbooks while encouraging waste and corruption. We are sick and tired of government promises of services that are never matched by performance. In this book we offer a simple, yet effective, alternative.

2

TAXPAYERS UNDER ATTACK

Benjamin Franklin wrote that "in this world, nothing is certain but death and taxes." Not much has changed in the two centuries since Franklin published *Poor Richard's Almanac*. Death and taxes are still among the few certainties. The only difference is that taxes have grown, and grown, and are still growing. But, crushing though taxes are, the total impact of government on the pocketbooks of its citizens is not fully recognized. Through regulation, government imposes indirect taxes on the public by forcing businesses to absorb higher costs, which are passed on in higher prices. Even that is not the whole story. Government has mortgaged our future by making commitments it can keep only by increasing taxes further. If Franklin's Poor Richard was impoverished in 1789, American taxpayers are in a bigger mess today and will be in worse shape tomorrow.

The Direct Burden of Government

Every level of government takes a large chunk out of the taxpayer's income. Local government demands the payment of real and personal property taxes, utility taxes, amusement taxes, hotel and restaurant taxes, licenses, permits, and fees of every sort and description. At the state level, sales taxes, income taxes, gasoline taxes, cigarette taxes, liquor taxes, unemployment taxes, and other sorts of levies proliferate. The federal government imposes income taxes, social-security taxes, excise taxes, import taxes; taxes on capital gains, windfall profits, and so forth. The existing array is mind-boggling.

The Tax Foundation, Inc., a nonprofit research organization, has developed one of the easiest ways to see this tax bite. Each year, the Tax Foundation computes Tax Freedom Day, the day of the year that the average worker can stop working for the government and start working to support himself and his family. In 1980, the average American spent 131 days working to pay taxes! Tax Freedom Day occurred on May 11. Government had taken 35.8 percent of the average worker's earnings—more than one dollar out of every three earned.[1]

Politicians keep bewailing the high cost of food and housing, and the cost of energy used in the home and in transportation. Those costs have risen and continue to rise. Yet the cost of these items, individually, is peanuts compared to the taxes we pay. Taxes take the largest proportion of the worker's income—more than any other single item—more than food, more than housing, more than transportation. In fact, the proportion of the eight-hour day required to pay taxes is larger than that needed for any two other items *combined*. The worker on a nine-to-five-thirty schedule must work almost until lunch to satisfy the local, state, and federal government's appetite for taxes. The data for 1979 are shown in Table 1.

Table 1

Tax Bite in the Eight-Hour Day for the
Average American Worker in 1979

Item	Hours and		Minutes	% of Time
Tax, federal	1 hour		47 minutes	22.3
Tax, state and local			58 minutes	12.1
Tax, total	2 hours		45 minutes	34.4
Food and beverages	1 hour		3 minutes	13.1
Housing/household operation	1 hour		27 minutes	18.1
Clothing			23 minutes	4.8
Transportation			42 minutes	8.8
Medical care			30 minutes	6.3
Recreation			19 minutes	4.0
All other*			51 minutes	10.5
	8 hours			100.0%

*The "all other" category includes expenditures for such items as personal care, personal business, education, and savings.

4

Most workers don't know how much of their money goes to government. Local, state, and federal income taxes and social-security taxes are "withheld" or deducted from the worker's paycheck. The worker never sees what is taken out. Sales and gasoline taxes are also "hidden" from the taxpayer because they are regarded as part of the "price" of the product. Even property taxes are often collected as part of the mortgage payment by a bank. If the American worker and consumer are feeling a budget "pinch" today, the pain is caused by government's appetite for taxes.

Over the years, government has become more and more greedy. In 1929, 39 days were required for the average worker to pay his taxes. Half a century later the tax bite had increased by 228 percent: 128 days of work were required to pay taxes in 1979. Tax Freedom Day is reported for various years in Table 2.[2]

Now, look at what's happened to the *distribution* of taxes between the federal government and the state and local governments! In 1929, out of each eight-hour day, the typical worker spent 19 minutes paying his federal tax bill and 33 minutes working for the state and local governments. Today this is reversed. Only 58 minutes of each eight-hour day are devoted to paying state and local taxes, but one hour and 47 minutes must be worked to satisfy the federal tax collector. Why is the shift of taxation from state and local governments to the federal

Table 2

Taxes as a Percent of Earnings and Tax Freedom Day for the Average Worker, by Decade
1929–1979

Year	Tax Freedom Day	Taxes as % of Earnings	Days Working for Government
1929	February 9	10.8	39
1939	March 5	17.4	63
1949	March 24	22.7	82
1959	April 15	28.6	104
1959	May 3	33.5	122
1978	May 6	34.3	125
1979	May 8	34.7	128
1980	May 11	35.8	131

government so important? The matter is simple. Taxes collected by local government are spent by local government. Because the taxpayer usually lives in the area in which local taxes are levied, the taxpayer can see more easily what benefits and services are received for tax dollars, if any. The closer the taxpayer is to government services, the more responsive is government itself to the public. Similarly, state tax revenues are generally spent within a state. Although more difficult than at the local level, it is still possible for a concerned and motivated taxpayer to find out what the government is doing to him or for him on the state level.

In contrast to the relative simplicity of state and local government, the operations of the federal government are a nightmare. The majority of state and local government revenues are spent on such things as education, roads and highways, and fire and police protection, which benefit the residents who pay the taxes. At the federal level, the link between who pays the taxes and who receives the benefits is far more remote. Citizens from one state may contribute far more tax dollars than are returned to the state in federal spending. The political process in Washington, D.C., is much more remote than the activities at the local city hall. It is impossible for any citizen—regardless of how motivated or concerned—to discover what nearly 2.5 million civilian employees of the federal government are doing, or not doing. As government becomes more centralized, the individual taxpayer has less to say about public decisions and is thereby more frustrated.

Both the tax take and the spending by government have soared in recent years, as shown in Table 3. Between 1950 and 1978, spending and taxes at all levels of government increased 10 times! Federal government spending increased almost as much between 1975 and 1978 as it did in the 20 years from 1950 to 1970.

Two factors help to explain some of the rapid rise in spending: inflation and population increases. Of course, not all government expenditures are directly affected by population growth. For example, water and sewer expenses would probably be affected, but expenditures for national defense would not. Even if adjustments are made for population growth (by placing spending and receipts on a per person basis) and for price rises (by using a price index to express receipts and expenditures in "constant dollars" over time), government at all levels has been one of the greatest growth "industries" of our age.

Table 3

Expenditures and Tax Receipts by Level of Government
Selected Years, 1950–1978

Year	Expenditure ($ Million)				Tax Receipts ($ Million)			
	Total	Federal	State	Local	Total	Federal	State	Local
1950	70,334	44,800	12,774	12,761	54,799	37,853	8,958	7,988
1955	110,717	73,441	17,400	19,875	87,915	63,291	12,735	11,890
1960	151,288	97,284	25,035	28,970	126,678	88,419	20,172	18,088
1965	205,682	130,059	35,726	39,897	165,475	111,231	29,120	25,124
1970	332,985	208,190	64,665	60,130	274,996	185,670	50,486	38,840
1975	560,129	340,542	122,153	97,434	413,941	267,321	85,290	61,330
1976	625,076	389,905	127,678	107,493	446,805	283,794	95,422	67,589
1977	680,329	430,594	137,683	112,052	523,193	338,754	109,608	74,831
1978	759,686	483,283	153,930	122,473	584,350	381,776	122,563	80,011

SOURCE: Tax Foundation, *Facts and Figures on Government Finance, 1979* (Washington, D.C.: Tax Foundation, 1979), pp. 17, 20.

7

Table 3 also shows that in every year, government expenditures exceeded tax receipts; the difference was made up in borrowing. By 1978, the gross debt of all levels of government had exceeded $1 trillion—an increase of more than 100 percent over the figure only 10 years earlier.[3] The gap between taxes and spending has also grown rapidly over time. In 1950, the difference was less that $16 billion. It had grown to more than $175 billion by 1978! If government were financed on a pay-as-you-go basis, the tax burden on individuals would be even greater.

The Indirect Burden of Government

The average worker turns over more than one-third of his earnings to various levels of government in taxes, but that is only the beginning. Government imposes many other costs on the taxpayer that are difficult to measure, but are very real. The income that remains after paying taxes to government is used by the consumer to buy goods and services. The prices we pay for goods and services have, in many cases, risen dramatically because of the regulatory activities of government. For example, consider a consumer who buys a new car. It is estimated that, because of federal regulations from 1968 to 1978, the cost of a new car has been pushed up by $665.87.[4]

Since approximately 10 million new cars and trucks are produced and purchased each year, government regulations have cost consumers about $6.7 billion.

Over the past 15 years, dozens of regulatory programs have been introduced. The rules and regulations are printed in the *Federal Register*. In 1970, the *Federal Register* was approximately 20,000 pages, but had mushroomed to more than 77,000 pages by the end of 1979. Keep in mind that these figures represent only federal government regulatory actions. State and local governments have also been swept by the epidemic of regulatory fever. A casual examination of the contents of the *Federal Register* boggles the mind. The federal government has dictated the shape of toilet seats, the size of knotholes permissible in wood used to build ladders, and the way in which stepladders may be climbed. Although the contents of some of the regulatory requirements may be comic (the Department of Health, Education, and Welfare does not allow words such as *man-made* in

8

its vocabulary), the price tag to U.S. consumers is not. One carefully developed estimate places the costs arising from federal regulation of business in 1979 at more than $102 billion—about $500 per person.[5]

As taxpayers, we must pay for government employees to write and enforce the regulations. As consumers we must pay higher prices for the products and services produced by regulated firms. Regulations are always justified on the basis of "protecting" the public safety, health, or pocketbooks. Yet, in spite of such claims, studies by a number of economists show that many regulations not only are costly, but also aren't worth a darn. For example, many of the price increases for new automobiles were caused by regulations related to automobile safety. Yet, a study at the University of Chicago has shown that these safety devices have had no effect whatever in reducing the death rate from automobile accidents, despite the billions of dollars spent by consumers.[6] The principal cause of automobile fatalities is the drunk driver—a problem that none of the regulations took into account.

The Occupational Safety and Health Administration was supposedly established to reduce hazards to workers on the job. Yet, a study reported that "what is clear is that the agency's enforcement policies have not had any direct impact on job hazards."[7]

The regulation of new drugs has sharply reduced the rate of innovation and introduction of effective new drugs to combat disease. Great Britain, where the drug environment is far less restrictive, has experienced marked benefits from new drugs that could not have been introduced in the U.S.[8] (Today, it would be difficult, if not totally impossible, to introduce such drugs as aspirin and penicillin, which have relieved millions from suffering and saved countless lives.)

Deregulation and the elimination of rigid government controls offer numerous benefits to taxpayers and consumers. Since the partial deregulation of the airlines by the Civil Aeronautics Board, consumers have benefited from lower fares and greater frequency of service resulting from heightened competition among airlines. The deregulation of the trucking industry, although strongly opposed by trucking firms and the truck drivers' union, will also benefit consumers by doing away with restrictive operating rules.

For example: one trucking company had permission to haul empty ginger ale bottles between Virginia and Pennsylvania, but could not carry empty cola or root beer bottles; another firm could ship five-gallon cans but not two-gallon cans (see "The Byzantine World of the

Trucking Industry," *Washington Post,* March 2, 1980, p. G1).

A second source of indirect costs of government is the paperwork and red tape associated with government forms. The nation is awash with bureaucratic forms! The Internal Revenue Service alone uses 13,200 forms, including form letters that are given form numbers; about 613 million man-hours were spent by individuals and businesses in fiscal year 1978 completing these forms. As of June 1972 the Office of Management and Budget reported that agencies of the federal government (excluding IRS) used 5,567 forms that generated more than 418 million responses.[9] The costs imposed on the private economy by this mountain of red tape, all passed on to the U.S. consumers, are enormous. Consider the following statement from the *Final Summary Report* of the U.S. Commission on Federal Paperwork, which was issued in October 1977:

> The total costs of federal paperwork are difficult to determine; but, as best we can estimate, more than $100 billion a year, or about $500 for each person in this country, is spent on federal paperwork. Our estimates of costs to some major segments of society are:
>
> - The federal government: $43 billion per year
> - Private industry: $25 to 32 billion per year
> - State and local government: $5 to 9 billion per year
> - Individuals: $8.7 billion per year
> - Farmers: $350 million per year
> - Labor organizations: $75 million per year[10]

The impact upon the economy of this volume of paperwork is terrible, particularly when we know that much of the information is redundant or not used. Firms, for example, must hire people to fill out forms and respond to the incessant demands of bureaucrats for data. When a firm's limited resources are diverted from production to filling out paperwork, the supply of consumer goods is reduced. The paperwork burden falls most heavily on the nation's small business enterprises—firms that cannot afford the specialized legal and clerical help needed to fill out many government forms. A businessman considering starting a new small business may be discouraged from doing so because the burden of paperwork is unmanageable. Existing firms may fail because they cannot cope with paperwork requirements. Paperwork thus contributes to the nation's unemployment problems, contributes to inflation, reduces the supply of goods and services available to the consumer, and makes American products less competitive in world markets. When the additional costs of local and state government paperwork are also taken into account, the total cost is horrendous!

It is clear that, if the indirect burdens of government were added to the direct burden, Tax Freedom Day would come much later in the year than May 11.

The Future Burden of Government

All the evidence shows that taxes will continue to increase. Governments have made enormous commitments of public funds for which there are not enough tax dollars to honor. For example, the largest tax increase ever enacted was passed in 1977 in an attempt to rescue the foundering social-security system. The Social Security Financing Act of 1977 guarantees that the taxes on workers will increase through the 1980s, as shown in Table 4.

The tax rate over 11 years rises from 5.85 to 7.15 percent, an increase of 22 percent. The maximum amount of earnings to be taxed also rises. So the minimum amount of tax that must be paid rises by 215 percent, from $965 to $3,046. If a worker's earnings follow the maximum taxable wage base, his income increases by a healthy 158 percent, but his social-security payments rise by more than 215 percent! And just think! These hefty raises in social-security taxes—amounting to $227 billion—are insufficient to keep the system healthy! As of September 20, 1978, the U.S. Treasury estimated that the social-security system still had a shortfall of $929 billion that would eventually have to be raised even after the 1977 tax increase.[11]

Military pensions also represent an enormous unfunded liability. During the 1970s the Department of Defense paid out $72 billion to retired servicemen, the majority of these funds going to able-bodied individuals in their 40s and 50s. The budget for fiscal year 1980 provides $11.5 billion for military pensions, a jump of 310 percent since 1970. Pensions alone account for almost 10 percent of the defense

11

Table 4

Social-Security Tax Rates, Taxable
Wage Base, and Tax Payments, by Year
1977–1987

Year	Tax Rate	Taxable Wage Base*	Maximum Tax
1977	5.85%	$16,500	$ 965.25
1978	6.05	17,700	1,070.85
1979	6.13	22,900	1,403.77
1980	6.13	25,900	1,587.67
1981	6.65	29,700	1,975.05
1982	6.70	31,800	2,130.60
1983	6.70	33,900	2,271.30
1984	6.70	36,000	2,412.00
1985	7.05	38,100	2,686.05
1986	7.15	40,200	2,874.30
1987	7.15	42,600	3,045.90

*The taxable wage base is established by statute through 1983; after that an automatic adjustment mechanism becomes effective. The wage base for 1984–87 is estimated.

budget. Because an individual in the military can receive a pension after only 20 years on active duty, regardless of age, recipients can expect to receive payments for a long period of time. The all-volunteer army, with its emphasis on pension benefits as a method of attracting and keeping servicemen, means that spending for military pensions will skyrocket! At the end of September 1978, unfunded obligations for retirement pay had already reached $225 billion.

It's the same with civil service pensions, although a federal government employee cannot receive a pension as early as a member of the armed services. The U.S. Treasury has estimated that the civil service pension system is underfunded to the tune of some $124 billion.

Continued inflation also guarantees that local, state, and federal governments will get a larger share of the worker's earnings. As wages rise, taxes rise, but by more than wages because income taxes are designed to be "progressive"; that is, as income rises, the tax *rate* increases. Even if the worker's salary keeps pace with inflation, he has less income to spend after taxes. Inflation also raises the value of

©MADHOUSE/THE BIKE

Form 1040

US Department of the Treasury — INTERNAL REVENUE SERVICE
Individual Income Tax Return

1976

FOR THE YEAR JANUARY 1 — DECEMBER 31, 1976, OR WHENEVER YOU GET AROUND TO IT

Please Type or Print

Name JEFF MACNELLY | Last Name MACNELLY | Second-to-Last Initial | STARCH? ☐ Yes ☐ No ☒

Present Address of Addressee (must be filled out by Addressee or legal Guardian or Aforementioned (unless greater than Line B above)
The RICHMOND NEWS LEADER | ☐ CUFFS ☐ NO CUT-S

City, Town, Post office, Shoe size (NO 12½) |

IS YOUR ADDRESS GREATER THAN LINE 4½? ☐ NO ☐ YES | OCCU-PATION ☐ YOURS ☐ SPOUSE

IF YES, WHY?

REQUESTED BY DEPARTMENT OF AGRICULTURE

A. HOW MANY TALKING CHICKENS DO YOU OWN? | D. Have you Rotated your Tires Lately? ☐ Yes ☐ No

B. NAMES | C. DO ANY OF THEM PLAY THE OBOE? ☐ Yes ☐ No

Q. DO YOU LIVE WITHIN 2 MILES OF A DECENT PIZZA PLACE? ☐ Yes ☐ No ☐ EXTRA CHEESE?

E. Yes? ☐ NO
F. No? ☐ YES

IF NO, FILE IRS Tire Rotation Schedule L

FOR IRS USE ONLY

YOU ARE Here →

Filing Status / Exemptions

1 ☐ Single ☐ Double ☐ Sacrifice Fly
2 ☐ Married Filing Singly Joint return (even IF SPOUSE IS MARRIED SEPARATELY)
3 ☐ Joint married singly separate spouse (but FILING DOUBLE JOINTED)
4 ☐ Head of Household filing separate but joint return (IF UNMARRIED BUT JOINTLY SINGLE)
5 ☐ Head of joint filing single file spouses separately
6 ☐ Widow(er) with separate dependent filing out of joint return singly

4 a Regular? ☐ yourself? ☐ Spouse ☐
  b Names of Dependent children who lived with you. . . . . Why?
  c Just First names Dummy. . . . .
4. Do you weigh more than last year's tax form?
  e Number of Parakeets subtracted from Gross Rotated Income (PLUS LINE 27 — UNLESS GREATER THAN TWELVE MILES)
  f How many inches in a liar?
7 a Total Confusion (add lines 6e AND f; g; fold in eggs, beat until firm). . . . . .

ENTER NUMBER OF BOXES CHECKED ▲
CHECK NUMBER OF BOXES ENTERED ▲
ENTER NUMBER OF CHECKED BOXERS ▲
DO NOTHING Here ▶

8 Presidential Election Campaign Fund ▶ DO YOU WISH TO DESIGNATE $1 OF YOUR TAXES TO THIS WORTHY CAUSE? . . . . ☐ Yes ☐ No
WHAT ABOUT THE LITTLE LADY? . . . . ☐ ISN'T THIS ☐ Yes NOTE: IF YOU CHECKED Yes, WE WILL COME AND STEAL ALL YOUR HUBCAPS ☐ No A DUMB LAW? ☐ No

9 Wages, Salaries, Tips, Extortion ◀ ATTACH W2 FORMS TO YOUR PORSCHE WITH HEAVY DUTY STAPLE GUN ▶ | 9.
10 Remunerations . . . . [IF LESS THAN GROSS REIMBURSEMENTS, THEN FILE SCHEDULE Q (See Page H of JOY OF COOKING") | 10.
11 Gross Influx . . . . . | 11.
12. Money you made . . . [IF $400 OR LESS, MORE OR LESS, LIST SCHEDULE B WITHOUT NOT FILING IN PART II AND R2, BUT MORE THAN LINE 3 | 12.
13. What about all that cash you stashed in that jar under the garage? ☐ Yes ☐ No
14. SUBTRACT 13 FROM 14
15. (THE ANSWER TO 15 IS . . . 1)

Think of a number between 1 and 10

• HOW WOULD YOU LIKE A GOOD SOCK IN THE FACE, FELLA? ☐ Yes ☐ No
• IF LINE 15 IS BIGGER THAN A BREADBOX OR MORE, GO TO LINE 43 TO FIGURE TAX | TAX RATE SCHEDULE X, Y, OR 12 ☐ See Page 7 of INSTRUCTIONS CHECK HERE ▶

here → or here | ← or here

real estate and personal property so that the tax take of local government also increases. The same is true of sales taxes.

If the taxpayer feels abused now, there is every indication that he'll feel worse in the future. Nevertheless, we believe that the real source of taxpayers' frustration is not so much that government is big, or even that it is growing rapidly, but that the taxpayer receives so little for his tax dollar.

What the Taxpayer Gets: Promises Versus Performance

At the federal level, billions of dollars are spent each year on housing and urban blight, on transportation programs, on energy programs, on poverty programs, and so on. Yet slums abound and the nation's cities continue to be filthy and to deteriorate. Urban transit can only be described as hopeless. The Department of Energy has not substantially reduced our dependence on imported oil. And the number of people in poverty seems never to decline. At the local and state levels of government, education, police protection, and road construction and maintenance are among the most important categories of spending. Yet, if national test scores of public school students are valid, public education is a mess. Crime rates in cities, suburbs, and even rural areas are soaring. The nation's roads and highways are full of potholes. Year after year, all levels of government have spent more and more to accomplish less and less.

Look at public education through high school. Table 5 contains some simple statistics on public school enrollment and revenue for selected school years between 1961 and 1978. Public school enrollment increased steadily through the 1971–72 school year and then began to decline. Revenues for public education, on the other hand, increased continually. Between academic years 1975–76 and 1977–78, total enrollment declined by more than one million students, while spending rose by over $10 billion. Only a small part of this increased spending can be attributed to inflation.

Since we taxpayers are paying more to educate fewer students, we should expect the quality of education to improve, right? Wrong! Between academic years 1961–62 and 1977–78, spending *per student* almost tripled, but national test scores over the period have *declined*.

14

Table 5

Public School Enrollment, Revenue, and
Revenue Per Student, Selected Years
1961–1978

School Year	Enrollment (Thousands)	Revenue (Millions)	$ Per Students	Scholastic Aptitude Test Verbal	Scholastic Aptitude Test Quantitative
1961–62	37,464	$17,527.7	$ 468	468	498
1963–64	40,187	20,420.0	500	475	498
1965–66	42,173	25,356.9	601	471	496
1967–68	43,891	31,903.1	727	466	494
1969–70	45,619	40,266.9	883	460	488
1971–72	46,081	50,003.7	1,085	453	484
1972–73	45,744	52,117.9	1,139	445	481
1973–74	45,429	58,230.9	1,282	444	480
1974–75	45,053	61,099.6	1,356	434	472
1975–76	44,791	70,802.8	1,580	431	472
1977–78	43,731	80,925.0	1,851	429	468

SOURCE: Tax Foundation, *Facts and Figures on Government Finance, 1979* (Washington, D.C.: Tax Foundation, 1979), pp. 255, 257.

15

The Scholastic Aptitude Test is given nationwide to high school graduates, usually those who desire to go to college, in order to test verbal and quantitative abilities. Average scores on these exams declined by 9.3 percent for the verbal portion of the test and by 6 percent for the quantitative portion. Public education has deteriorated to the point that some states have even passed laws requiring students to pass basic literacy exams before they can graduate from high school! No wonder more and more Americans are calling for a tax revolt.

The Tax Revolt

The tax revolt has been dramatized by the passage of Proposition 13 in California in June 1978. The rebellion of the taxpayers against higher taxes began much earlier with voter rejection of local bond issues in numerous states. But California's tax revolt received particular notoriety because it was the first successful statewide public protest over tax matters and because of the personality of Howard Jarvis. Since the passage of Proposition 13, a number of other states have adopted various types of tax limitation laws and about 30 states have adopted resolutions calling for a constitutional convention to draft an amendment requiring a balanced federal budget.

The message is clear: Voters believe they are not getting their money's worth from tax dollars. Tax limitation and reduction are the voters' protest against government expansion and waste. By limiting the income of government, voters are trying to restrain government expansion and to make the public sector more cost-conscious.

A much more dramatic action against government has apparently been taken by millions of workers: they have stopped paying taxes altogether! The Internal Revenue Service has long recognized that some income is not reported by moonlighting workers, illegal aliens, retailers who "skim" sales, and individuals and firms that trade goods and services. Until recently, IRS has maintained that the amount of untaxed income earned in the "underground economy" was very small. To admit otherwise would have raised questions about the agency's ability to collect taxes and might also have given other unhappy taxpayers undesirable ideas about paying taxes to the federal government.

16

In September 1979 IRS reversed its position and issued an extensive report, "Estimates of Income Unreported on Individual Tax Returns." It was estimated that taxpayers failed to report between $100 and $135 billion dollars in legal and illegal income in 1976. Another study by Professor Peter Gutmann of Baruch College arrived at approximately the same figure.[12] A more sophisticated and detailed analysis was undertaken to demonstrate that these estimates by IRS and Gutmann were too high.[13] Instead, that study revealed that the underground economy was much larger than originally thought and was growing fast. In 1976 unreported income was estimated at $369.1 billion and had nearly doubled to $704.4 billion by 1978. The tax revolt is bigger than ever before realized. Millions of people are so fed up with taxes and government waste that they just refuse to report income and pay taxes.

Conclusion

If public confidence in government is to be restored, the tax burden must be reduced and public services produced efficiently. It is clear that the waste, corruption, and inefficiency associated with government programs are no longer tolerable.

NOTES TO CHAPTER 2

[1]Tax Foundation, "May 11 Is Tax Freedom Day," *Monthly Tax Features* (April 1980), pp. 1–2.

[2]*Ibid.*, p. 2.

[3]Tax Foundation, *Facts and Figures on Government Finance, 1979* (Washington, D.C.: Tax Foundation, 1979), p. 22.

[4]Murray L. Weidenbaum, *The Future of Business Regulation* (New York: Amacom Books, 1979), p. 13.

[5]*Ibid.*, pp. 22–23.

[6]Sam Peltzman, "The Effects of Automobile Safety Regulation," *Journal of Political Economy* (August 1975): pp. 677–725.

[7]W. Kip Viscusi, "The Impact of Occupational Safety and Health Regulation," *Bell Journal of Economics* (Spring 1979): p. 136.

[8]Sam Peltzman, "The Benefits and Costs of New Drug Development," *Regulating New Drugs*, ed. Richard Landau (Chicago: University of Chicago Center for Policy Study, 1973), pp. 9–20; see also Peltzman, *Regulation of Pharmaceutical Innovation: The 1962 Amendments* (Washington, D.C.: American Enterprise Institute for Public

Policy Research, 1974), and William Wardell, "Therapeutic Implications of the Drug Lag," *Clinical Pharmacology and Therapeutics* (January 1974): pp. 73–96.

[9]For a detailed discussion of federal paperwork, see James T. Bennett and Manuel H. Johnson, "The Political Economy of Federal Government Paperwork," *Policy Review* (Winter 1979): pp. 27–43.

[10]U.S. Comission on Federal Paperwork, *Final Summary Report* (Washington, D.C.: U.S. Government Printing Office, 1977), p. 5.

[11]Fiscal Service, U.S. Treasury, Bureau of Government Financial Operations, "Statement of Liabilities and Other Financial Commitments of the United States Government as of September 30, 1978," p. 24.

[12]Peter M. Gutmann, "Statistical Illusions, Mistaken Policies," *Challenge* (November–December 1979), pp. 5–13.

[13]Edgar L. Feige, "How Big Is the Irregular Economy?" *Challenge* (November–December 1979), pp. 5–13.

3

WHY BUREAUCRATS BUNGLE

As every taxpayer knows, government is wasteful and inefficient; it always has been and always will be. More than 70 years ago, President Theodore Roosevelt stated in his seventh annual message to Congress that throughout the federal government, "antiquated practices and bureaucratic ways have been abolished, and a general renovation of departmental methods has been inaugurated."[1] Despite such sweeping claims, every president since Teddy Roosevelt has promised reform of the federal government as part of his campaign platform. President Carter promised to "reorganize" government and won support with his "anti-Washington" stance. Nothing much has changed, however, except that two new cabinet-level departments (Energy and Education) have been created. Nothing effective seems to have been done to end endless red tape, regulations, paperwork, and inefficiency and waste in government operations.

Starting in 1887, a host of agencies, boards, bureaus, committees, commissions, departments, and task forces have undertaken appraisals, analyses, hearings, investigations, and studies that have resulted in directives, executive orders, legislation, reports, and recommendations to reduce federal paperwork. The congressional hearings that continue today only expose the ineffectiveness of past efforts.[2] Regulations and red tape continue to proliferate. There are numerous reports of fraud, corruption, bribes, kickbacks, boondoggles, and waste. State and local governments have the same problems.

People who are employed by local, state, and federal governments are sometimes referred to as public employees, civil servants, or public servants, but in the mind of the frustrated taxpayer, the appropriate term is *bureaucrat*. The terms *bureaucrat* and *bureaucracy* have long

19

been used to identify the worst aspects of government employees and organizations: paperwork, red tape, regulations, waste, and inefficiency. Everyone is convinced that bureaucracy is bad and would not exist in a perfect world. No one wants to be referred to as a bureaucrat or to have his methods and procedures of management labeled bureaucratic.[3]

It is tempting to blame the bureaucrat for the problems so common at all levels of government. But public employees as *individuals* are not at fault. When someone goes to work in government, he is not issued a halo, nor does he grow a set of horns. The same is true of those who work in private enterprise: they are inherently neither saints nor sinners. Instead, all people are the same in that they respond to incentives: they seek rewards and avoid punishments. In both the public and the private sector, managers and workers will do things that will increase their salary, position, and prestige and will avoid doing things that will result in pay cuts and demotions.

The incentives in the public sector and in the private sector are very different. By studying these incentives, it is easy to understand why government so often fails and private firms succeed.

Incentives: The Public Sector

Incentives usually consist of two parts: the "carrot" of reward for good performance and the "stick" of punishment for poor performance. Unfortunately, neither the carrot nor the stick is present in government bureaucracies.

With regard to the stick, the most powerful motive for good performance, the threat of dismissal, is largely absent for lazy or incompetent workers. It is all but impossible to fire an employee of the federal government. The chairman of the Consumer Product Safety Commission described the frustrations of the termination process in a letter to Sen. Charles Percy of Illinois:

> A manager in the executive branch of the federal government who finds it necessary to terminate an unproductive or noncontributing employee—or even an obstructing employee—must be prepared to spend 25 percent to 50 percent of his time for a period that may run from six to 18 months.

> In many cases, managers have chosen to work around such
> a person or to promote the employee out of the office in
> order to quickly be rid of the problem.[4]

That's why firing government workers rarely occurs. Instead, incompetent employees can be given *promotions* because it is easier to promote them to another position to get rid of them than to kick them out. To a large degree, the same difficulties are present in state and local governments as well. If an employee cannot be dismissed and may be rewarded for incompetence, why should a lazy employee try to do his best?

Equally important, the bureaucracy has no reason to fear that competitors will drive the public firm out of business by offering better service at a lower price. By government mandate, the public firm enjoys a monopoly. The U.S. Postal Service, that paragon of inefficiency, is given exclusive rights by law to deliver certain types of mail and has used its authority to stop private firms from competing. There are cases in which private enterprises do compete directly with the public sector—for example, private and public schools. But no real competition exists because the taxpayer is forced to support the public school whether he likes it or not. If parents send their children to private schools, they still have to pay the same level of taxes to support the public schools. The only alternative is to move away—but where?

If a public employee is inefficient or incompetent, he has little to fear from his superiors or from competitors. The stick of punishment, for all practical purposes, does not exist in a government bureaucracy.

Nor are there any real incentives for efficient performance and cost reduction. The only income for the bureaucrat is the fixed salary from his job. If, by extra effort, he achieves cost reductions, he doesn't get a bonus or raise. His salary is not related in any way to saving tax dollars. He has, therefore, no reason to be particularly efficient or cost-conscious. In any case, it would be very difficult to increase efficiency, since it is not possible to eliminate deadwood employees.

Although the bureaucrat cannot increase his salary by saving taxpayer dollars, it is possible to obtain other benefits from government employment. In addition to a relaxed pace, bureaucrats love to travel at taxpayer expense to meetings, conferences, and the like. Senator James Sasser of Tennessee has estimated that at any given moment, there are 20,000 bureaucrats aloft in airplanes and the federal travel budget alone is nearly $8 billion! Much of this travel is unnecessary and, as is repeatedly pointed out in the media, conferences are frequently held in Hawaii, the Virgin Islands, and other resort and sightseeing locales.

There is worse to come! Each government bureau is appropriated an annual budget by the Congress, the legislature, or the city council. If the bureau saves money, some funds are left over at the end of the year, a rare occurrence. Bureaucrats make every effort to make sure that all allocated funds are spent by the end of the budget year, so there is a wild spending spree as each fiscal year draws to a close. Some examples:

1. In fiscal year 1978, the Department of Health, Education, and Welfare obligated $572 million or 21 percent of its annual contract money during September, the final month of the fiscal year.
2. The secretary of HEW obligated 77 percent of the annual printing budget for his office in September 1978.
3. A September 1978 memo to the commissioner of education indicated that $2 million could be "declared surplus" to allocate as he saw fit. His assistant advised that "we need to move quickly as these funds lapse at midnight September 30."
4. The Department of Housing and Urban Development obligated 49 percent of its total gross obligations in September 1978 on such items as $35,000 worth of wooden desks . . . which were still in storage in original shipping cartons in August 1979.[5]

Why are bureaucrats so anxious not to return leftover funds at the end of the year? The reason is simple: it would be hard to ask for more money for the following year if all funds requested for the current year had not been spent. Government employees are driven to increase the agency's budget each year because a bureaucrat in the United States (and in Western Europe as well) is rewarded with higher rank, increased salary, and greater prestige for increasing the number of employees under him. To hire additional employees, additional appropriations

22

must be obtained to pay their salaries. The very nature of bureaucracy provides powerful incentives for increasing the size and scope of government. Every bureaucrat is by nature an empire builder.

But what about the individual taxpayer and private firms? First, their tax burden increases as funds must be raised to pay for an expanding public sector. Second, indirect costs are passed on to the public in the form of additional paperwork, regulations, and red tape. These additional costs make U.S. firms less competitive in world markets, encourage imports as substitutes for more expensive domestic goods, and contribute to the problems of unemployment and inflation.

Why, then, don't our politicians control the purse strings and root out inefficiency and waste? The major concern of every politician is getting elected and reelected to public office. Successful politicians do not antagonize well-organized and powerful groups of voters. Government employees form an impressive voting group not only because of their large numbers—there are 2.5 million full-time federal civilian employees—but also because they are politically aware. Studies have shown that bureaucrats are more likely to vote than other eligible citizens (government employees are usually given time off to go to the polls) and therefore have an important impact on the outcomes of elections.[6] Further, organizations of public employees, such as fire and police unions and the local and state associations of teachers, provide campaign funds to candidates for public office; these organizations are unlikely to support candidates who make life difficult for their members.

The bureaucracy can also "retaliate" against a politician who is uncooperative. One of the most important functions of a public official is to provide services for constituents. One of these services is to help constituents in dealing with government agencies. Most of the staff of senators and congressmen are involved in unraveling bureaucratic foulups with social-security checks, medicare-medicaid payments, welfare payments, and so forth. If a politician supports an agency, complaints and requests can be expedited and easily resolved, but if the bureaucrats believe a politician is a troublemaker, his constituents may suffer, and, at election time, the politician may pay the price. Finally, because government agencies have a monopoly on the services they provide, the threat of a strike or work slowdown can be very unsettling—there are no alternative sources of supply. Thus, if a politician attempts to cut budgets or personnel of an agency, he risks angering both the public employees and the voters.

Even if a politician wanted to reduce government, it would be all but impossible to do so. Government agencies, especially at the federal level, are large and complicated. The employees of agencies can number in the tens of thousands and the budget in the tens of billions. Politicians have neither the time nor the staff resources to delve deeply into the operations of federal agencies to expose waste and corruption. Politicians also become advocates of government programs: senators and congressmen from farm states attempt to be assigned to committees dealing with agriculture; those from urban areas are interested in committees dealing with housing and transportation. Once a politician advocates spending for a program to aid his constituents (and his chances for reelection), it is not in his self-interest to publicize the failures and shortcomings of the program. For these reasons, the checks politicians are supposed to have to make sure that the taxpayer gets full value for his tax dollar just do not work.

Most politicians also support the expansion of government because they, like the bureaucrats, benefit from it. New government programs create patronage positions that can be used to reward supporters and pork-barrel spending that can be distributed to constituents.[7] One measure of the "effectiveness" of a politician is how well he manages to bring home the bacon for those he represents. In fairness, we recognize that there are people in Congress who are aware of the bloated bureaucracy and who try to reduce costly paperwork and burdensome regulation. On the whole, however, they are the exceptions.

Although both bureaucrats and politicians may strongly favor the growth of new government programs, there is the risk of a taxpayer revolt if taxes must be increased to pay for the increased spending. The appropriations which fuel government growth are limited by tax revenues and the size of the deficit that can be financed without a public uproar. Two factors have lowered resistance of voters to a rapid increase in spending: the more relaxed attitude toward government deficits (a legacy of the Keynesian tradition), and inflation. James Buchanan and Richard Wagner have dealt with the role of deficit finance in detail in their excellent book *Democracy in Deficit*.[8] Inflation helps fill the coffers of government treasuries without the politically explosive problem of a tax rate increase. As incomes and property

24

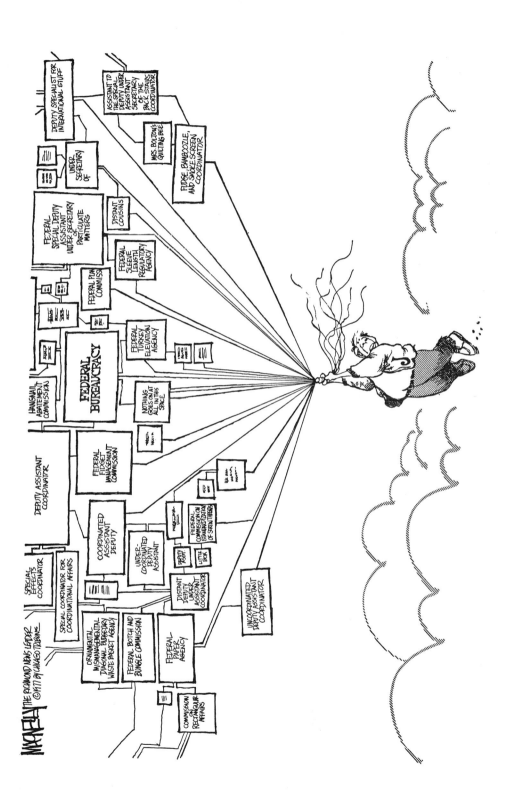

values rise because of inflation, the tax take of government rises; in the case of income taxes, the rise is steeper because of the progressive nature of the income tax.

How do politicians keep on adding more and more expensive programs to government and still avoid the wrath of the taxpayer? The solution is simple: convince the voter that a new government program is absolutely essential and that dire consequences will result unless it is instituted. In short, the public must be convinced that a crisis exists, for a crisis implies catastrophic consequences for the country unless dramatic changes are made quickly. Examples of such "crises" are commonplace: the energy crisis, the health-care crisis, the environmental crisis, and even the crisis of "confidence." The crisis may be real or imaginary—all that is required is that the public be convinced that the costs of the new program are small compared to the benefits gained by dealing with it.

If the politician perceives that there is organized support or little real opposition to a new program, the reluctance to appropriate funds can easily be overcome. The dramatization of the crisis immediately mobilizes interest groups that may benefit from the spending and regulations that accompany new bureaucratic programs. For example, consulting companies know that new programs will require studies and reports; private businesses may benefit from increased sales— manufacturers of pollution-control equipment found a bonanza in the programs of the Environmental Protection Agency and coal producers were heartened by the "energy crisis." Such interest groups rally quickly to lobby for the passage of the new program and the politician finds an additional source of campaign contributions and votes at election time.

The news media cooperate willingly in selling the crisis to the public. After all, crises sell newspapers and guarantee high ratings for news broadcasts. Pending doom and disaster have always been the stock-in-trade of newspapers, radio, and television. Since recorded history, plagues, earthquakes, war, and other cataclysmic events have always captured the imagination.

You may ask, If the crises that the bureaucracy exploits are more contrived than real, why does the taxpayer continue to accept the bureaucrat's interpretation of events? Is the public so gullible or ignorant that bureaucratic claims continue to be accepted without serious question? Well, first, and most important, when advocating a new

26

government program, the fact that new jobs and opportunities for promotion exist in the bureaucracy is never mentioned as one of the "benefits." Rather, the "public servant" claims to be acting solely in the "public interest" and against private malefactors. For example, the "greed" of the OPEC nations and the oil companies is the cause of the energy crisis; profiteering by industry is the source of pollution; food price rises are caused by the "gouging" of middlemen. Claims of innocence by those accused have little, if any, impact. Their position is seen as self-serving and therefore biased. In sum, one reason that the assertions made by bureaucrats are credible is that the motives of the private sector are called into question. Those who benefit from the expansion of the public sector have found it useful to undermine public confidence in private enterprise.

Much is made of the powerful lobbies of industries, companies, and private-interest groups. Yet, one rarely hears about the numerous and very well financed lobbying efforts of nearly every agency of government. The lobbying efforts of the bureaucracy make the spending of private-sector firms and trade associations seem trivial. Agencies spend enormous amounts of time, effort, and (at the federal level) close to half a billion taxpayer dollars each year lobbying for ever greater spending.[9]

A second reason for public acceptance of bureaucratic crises is the complexity of the issues involved. Few Americans understand even the most basic principles of nuclear-power generation or the requirements for nuclear safety. The exploration for and the production and distribution of oil and natural gas are far beyond the expertise of most people. Further, most of us cannot spend the time and effort required to obtain detailed information about a wide variety of specialized fields. Thus, it is not surprising that the public so often accepts the views publicized by the bureaucracy.

People fear what they do not understand and one of the greatest fears in the American psyche is cancer. The Food and Drug Administration and the Environmental Protection Agency have ably exploited this fear. The list of suspected carcinogens is long and rapidly growing. Whenever public or political interest in one of these two agencies seems to be waning, a new suspect is announced. In August 1979 the FDA even determined that Scotch whisky and beer contained carcinogens, but, fortunately, the concentrations are so small that cirrhosis of the liver is a greater risk than cancer, thus negating major concern.

Prior to its appropriation hearings before Congress several years ago, the EPA announced that drinking water in America caused cancer, but then reversed itself and asserted that only in New Orleans was there a serious problem. Products accused of causing cancer are of course, banned, with the exception of cigarettes. The link between smoking and cancer is probably stronger than in any other case, but no one in government strongly advocates a ban, simply because there are too many addicted voters and too many tobacco farmers who vote—besides, cigarettes are heavily taxed and are a healthy source of revenue.

Once an appropriation has been approved for a new program, a staff is hired, offices acquired, and the bureau undertakes various activities. However, it is useful to pass as much of the cost of the agency as possible on to the private sector so that the public funds appropriated for the agency can be used for perquisites. Forms and paperwork are ideal for this purpose, since the agency can compel private firms to spend millions of man-hours responding to incessant demands for information at no cost to itself. Private contractors with the federal government are permitted to include the cost of filling out forms as part of overhead costs and be reimbursed for doing so. Ultimately, the taxpayers pay these costs and, as consumers, must also bear the costs of the paperwork blizzard on firms that produce goods and services for the private sector. By producing paper, the bureau can convince the politician who appropriated the funds that the agency is actively pursuing its goals, and at the same time pass the costs on to the private sector. When this occurs, private-sector labor and resources are confiscated by the bureaucracy and the true cost of government is concealed.

Although bureaucrats have a vested interest in identifying or creating a crisis, obtaining public support for it, and convincing the politician to appropriate funds to "do" something about the crisis, there is nothing whatever to be gained from actually solving or alleviating any problem on the national, state, or local level of government. If any crisis is solved, the bureaucrat's job and perhaps the entire agency's existence are in danger. If appropriations are to increase, crises must multiply. As in *Catch-22*, bureaucratic failure is, for the bureaucrat, success.

Thus, DOE makes no progress in dealing with energy; HEW has no incentive to get recipients off welfare; the FDA will continue to

28

find new carcinogens; and the EPA will press for additional controls and constraints to combat pollution. Once the incentive structure of bureaucrats and politicians is understood, it is easy to explain why taxpayers always pay more and get less from government.

The Energy Crisis and Bureaucratic Incentives

Now let us consider the nation's "energy crisis." In late 1973 the Arab oil embargo caused a temporary interruption in the supply of imported crude oil to the United States. Immediately the government began to project visions of Americans shivering in darkened homes and automobiles and trucks stranded by lack of fuel. (The trucks naturally would be trying to deliver food and medical supplies.) A Federal Energy Office was rapidly established and given broad powers to allocate fuel supplies. Long lines formed at gasoline stations, particularly on the East Coast and the Washington, D.C., area. The message to the politicians that a crisis existed was loud and clear. It was soon argued that a more "comprehensive" federal energy policy was necessary, and the Federal Energy Administration was created. As expected, "more comprehensive" implied that additional appropriations and staff were required to "coordinate" activities. Long-range "planning" was deemed essential. Although it is now largely forgotten, the FEA was scheduled to be disbanded as soon as the crisis was resolved. However, to no one's surprise, the FEA was so unequal to the task that in October 1977, it was succeeded by the Department of Energy. This cabinet-level agency had a budget well in excess of $10 billion and more than 20,000 employees in fiscal 1978.

The performance of this agency and its predecessors can only be described as dismal. At the outset, the goal of energy policy was self-sufficiency (remember Project Independence?). The idea was to make the U.S. independent of unreliable foreign energy sources by 1980, undoubtedly an overly ambitious objective. But considering the vast sums of money spent, the hordes of employees, and the extensive regulatory authority granted to the energy agencies, one might reasonably have expected, if not total self-sufficiency, at least some progress toward this goal. At the end of 1978, only a year from the target date for energy independence, political instability in Iran produced an interruption in imports of crude oil to the U.S. In total volume, these imports represented somewhere between three and five percent of our supplies. After five years of "planning," that loss should have caused only a minor ripple in the energy sector.

Instead, chaos. Long gas lines developed—again in the nation's capital. Nonsensical and conflicting statements were issued by the Department of Energy about supplies, consumption, and allocations. The bureaucratic response was immediate: a call for rationing, the imposition of mandatory thermostat settings, and, of course, the insistence that additional funding was required to cope with the crisis and to hire staff. OPEC was blamed for higher prices and oil companies were chastised for withholding supplies, for greed and excess profits, and for misleading the public.

There were problems, but they traced to bureaucratic bungling. It was difficult for the bureaucracy to advocate rationing, for DOE was two years late in developing a rationing plan to submit to Congress. Similarly, the development of a "strategic reserve" to cushion the U.S. against temporary interruptions in supply was also behind schedule. Thousands of barrels of oil were being pumped into salt domes for storage, but no one, apparently, had bothered to install pumps to get the oil out in time of need. Nor was a distribution system operating; even if the oil could have been pumped to the surface, it could not have been brought to market. Hence, the strategic reserves were useless.

Amid this ballyhoo, the real solution to the nation's energy crisis appeared on our doorstep. An energy bonanza of oil and gas was being developed in Mexico. So enormous are Mexico's reserves that this country is believed to rival, if not equal, Saudi Arabia in recoverable supplies of petroleum products. The output could easily exceed the domestic needs of Mexico, and this friendly neighbor is so close that oil would not have to be tankered for thousands of miles around the world through insecure sea lanes. Overland pipelines could be built to reduce transport cost and ensure a reliable source of supply. The U.S. energy shortage, it seemed, could be solved for years to come. So what did the energy bureaucrats do? The oil bonanza offered by Mexico was treated as a catastrophe! The secretary of energy, with bureaucratic retinue in tow, flew to Mexico for "talks" on energy

30

issues. Even though the U.S. was still deep in the grips of the "crisis" caused by Iran, no agreements of any sort were reached and hard feelings replaced a traditional spirit of cooperation. There were to be no quick solutions to the energy crisis from that quarter. Even today, only token amounts of natural gas and only a trickle of crude oil are being imported from Mexico. The Department of Energy, after spending billions of dollars and tens of thousands of man-years of effort, has not yet produced a single drop of oil or a single major success in dealing with energy problems.

Incentives: The Private Sector

In contrast to the public sector, both the carrot of reward and the stick of punishment fully operate in private enterprise. Managers have to produce goods and services of quality acceptable to the consumer at the lowest possible price. In the private sector, a manager's performance and prospects for future promotions are often directly related to the profits attained by the organization he manages. Bonus plans, which permit him to increase his income by increasing profits, are very common in industry. Profits can be increased by cost cutting. To increase income, the manager is motivated to be as efficient as possible. In addition, an incompetent or lazy worker can be demoted or fired. Hard work and productive effort are rewarded and incompetence punished in the private sector.

What *guarantees* that efficiency will exist in the private sector? Suppose that a company's management decides to tolerate waste and inefficiency; what will correct such a situation? The market. In the private economy, firms have competition from both domestic and foreign firms that produce similar products. If a company becomes lax in its management, costs will begin to rise. If prices are not increased for the goods and services produced by the company, profits will fall and, eventually, losses will be incurred. A firm cannot sustain losses for long and still remain in business. Therefore, even if inefficient managers are tolerated, their inefficiency will be punished when the losses cause the firm to go broke. They will lose their jobs.

An alternative to reduced profits is for the managers of the company to try to pass on the costs of inefficient operation to its customers

31

through higher prices. But, as prices increase, consumers can switch to similar products made by other companies. In some instances, the number of substitutes may be quite limited, as in the case of highly concentrated industries or single sources of supply such as electric utilities or natural-gas companies. As prices rise, however, consumers respond by buying less of the product, and, for example, by switching to wood stoves for heat. Even private monopolies are not wholly insulated from the discipline of the market. If price increases are used to offset the costs of inefficient management, the firm risks losing customers and revenues to competing companies and products. The result is the same: the firm may be driven from the marketplace if losses are incurred. In simple terms, efficiency is required for survival in the private sector.

The market mechanism also keeps in check the temptation of managers in efficient firms to raise profits by reducing the quality of the goods and services produced. Here again is the risk that consumers will switch to alternative sources of supply provided by existing or new firms or to competing products. The ability of the private firm to manipulate prices and quality is held in check by the ever-present threat of competition. Many firms in many industries have found, to their dismay, that the customer is both demanding and fickle. When car buyers discovered that U.S. auto manufacturers were not producing the compact cars they desired, foreign companies captured a big share of the market; a large portion of the steel, textiles, and electronic equipment consumed in the U.S. is also produced by foreign firms.

The Optimal Scale of Operations:
Public Versus Private Enterprise

Aside from incentives, there is another important economic reason why private firms produce goods and services at a lower cost than public firms. Public firms generally provide services to an entire state, city, county, or the nation. Private firms, however, don't have to stay within political boundaries. Many private firms operate in more than one political jurisdiction or even nationwide. The cost per unit of producing a particular good or service often varies with the size of the market served. If costs per unit decline as the number of units produced increases, "economies of scale" are said to exist; "diseconomies of scale" are present when costs per unit increase as the size of the market increases.

Private firms are free to adjust the scale of operations so that the minimum cost of production per unit can be achieved. If scale economies are present, the firm may expand by serving a larger market to benefit from these economies; alternatively, the private firm may remain small to avoid the additional costs or diseconomies associated with greater output. The reason there are no "mom-and-pop" steel companies, aluminum smelters, or automobile stamping plants is that economies of scale are present: as more is produced, the cost per unit falls. The cost per unit for a very small company would be so high that it could not compete. Similarly, there are no nationwide barbershops, sporting goods stores, laundries, or gift shops because diseconomies of scale exist; when diseconomies are present, many small competing firms exist side by side. A large firm may serve a national or even a worldwide market. A small firm may serve a market limited to a few square miles or to a few city blocks.

In contrast, public enterprises must serve the entire political jurisdiction; the political boundaries of the market for the public enterprise are far more likely to be the result of historical accident or geography than of economic planning. A glance at any map of the United States reveals a crazy-quilt pattern of wildly different shapes and sizes. Alaska is more than twice as large as Texas in land area; at least nine states are smaller than one county in Nevada (Nye County has more than 18 thousand square miles). Some cities have areas of only one or two square miles. Terrain can also influence the provision of services; states and counties can be split by mountain ranges, deserts, and bodies of water. Some states and counties are oddly shaped with "panhandles"—Maryland, Texas, and Oklahoma, for example. Far-reaching extensions of territory make the efficient provision of services more difficult than if the service area were tightly clustered geographically.

In addition to the area served and its geography, the distribution of service units within the market area can influence costs. Population density can influence the efficiency of services as well. Some areas are very sparsely populated while others have high concentrations of people. In New York State, Hamilton County has a density of fewer than three persons per square mile, whereas almost 1.5 million people lived in the 23 square miles of New York City proper in 1975. Thus, even within the borders of a single state, population density can vary widely.

A political entity may be so large that diseconomies occur when service is provided for the entire area or it may be so small that it may not be possible to realize the benefits of economies of scale. Further, because of technological change and innovation in production methods, minimum cost of output for a service can easily change over time. Political entities cannot adjust to such changes.

Even though a political jurisdiction may, by accident, be of ideal size for the production of a particular good or service, it is impossible for the public sector to produce *all* goods and services at lowest cost, for two reasons. First, all goods and services produced by the government are not subject to identical scale economies. In other words, a public firm that is of ideal size to produce service X at minimum cost may be too large to produce service Y or too small to produce service Z efficiently. Economists have done much research on whether or not economies of scale are present for various goods and services produced by the public sector.[10] This research has shown that unit costs fall as the scale of operation increases for water, sewer, and electric services. Thus, these three services can be produced efficiently by a public firm only if the size of the political jurisdiction or the market served is very large. The reverse is true for police, primary and secondary education, and refuse collection. Unit costs do not fall much, if at all, as the number served increases.

Second, economies and diseconomies of scale apply to the *financing* as well as to the *production* of a good or service. A political jurisdiction may be too small to use cost-cutting techniques to collect fees for a service or to get favorable terms for borrowing to finance capital equipment.

To produce and finance public services at minimum cost, it would be necessary to have two different sizes of political jurisdictions for each public service: one to minimize the cost of finance and the other to minimize the cost of production. Such a system would undoubtedly lead to massive inefficiencies. The voters would be hopelessly confused by overlapping political units and the potential for community participation would be lost as would any notion of local identity.

34

Some attempts have been made to "consolidate" political units to produce certain public services. One example is the consolidation of school districts throughout the United States. The total number of school districts fell from 117,018 in 1939–40 to less than 18,000 in 1970–71. The predictable result of such consolidations has been an increase in the number of administrative personnel and a huge increase in salaries. There is no evidence that the costs of education have been reduced or that a higher quality of education has resulted.[11] A second example is the Washington, D.C., subway system, Metro. A number of different political jurisdictions are "cooperating" to finance and construct the 100-mile subway system. From the outset, the project has been plagued with lengthy delays, enormous cost overruns, and political bickering. No acceptable means have been found to finance the system's operating deficits. One of the smallest participants, Fairfax City, with a population of less than 25,000, has been a maverick in the subway project. This city will not enjoy the benefits of having a subway stop and has resisted pressures to accept various plans to finance a subway system that does not serve its citizens. When fares on buses operated by Metro authorities were raised, Fairfax City chartered its own bus fleet (at a much lower cost) from a private company. Though consolidation may seem an attractive way to produce or finance public services, in practice this dream is generally a nightmare.

NOTES TO CHAPTER 3

[1]See U.S. Commission on Federal Paperwork, *What the Federal Government Has Tried to Do About Paperwork: A Technical Report of the Commission on Federal Paperwork* (Washington, D.C.: U.S. Government Printing Office, 1977), p. 3–1.

[2]The paperwork problem in the federal bureaucracy has been addressed in detail by James T. Bennett and Manuel H. Johnson, "Paperwork and Bureaucracy," *Economic Inquiry* (July 1979): pp. 435–51, and by the same authors in "The Political Economy of Federal Government Paperwork," *Policy Review* (Winter 1979): pp. 27–43.

[3]One of the earliest studies of the economic behavior of bureaucracy was written in 1944 by Ludwig von Mises. Even then, the negative connotations of the terms *bureaucrat* and *bureaucracy* were pervasive. See Ludwig von Mises, *Bureaucracy* (New Haven: Yale University Press, 1944), p. 1.

[4]Joel Havemann, "Can Carter Chop Through the Civil Service System?" *National Journal* (April 24, 1977), p. 619.

[5]U.S. Congress, House Committee on Post Office and Civil Service, "Federal

Personnel Ceilings and Contracting Activities," Report 96–729 (Part 1) (December 20, 1979), p. 13.

[6]Winston Bush and Arthur Denzau, "The Voting Behavior of Bureaucrats and Public Sector Growth," *Budgets and Bureaucrats: The Sources of Government Growth*, ed. Thomas Borcherding (Durham, N.C.: Duke University Press, 1977), pp. 90–99.

[7]Two of the most perceptive writers on the behavior of bureaucrats and politicians are Paul Craig Roberts and Gordon Tullock. See, for example, Paul Craig Roberts, "Idealism in Public Choice Theory," *Journal of Monetary Economics* (August 1978) p. 605; "The Political Economy of Bureaucratic Imperialism," *The Intercollegiate Review* (Fall 1976) pp. 3–11; and Roberts and Alvin Rabushka, "A Diagrammatic Exposition of an Economic Theory of Imperialism," *Public Choice* (Spring 1973) pp. 101–7. See also Gordon Tullock, *The Politics of Bureaucracy* (Washington, D.C.: Public Affairs Press, 1965).

[8]James M. Buchanan and Richard E. Wagner, *Democracy in Deficit* (New York: Academic Press, 1977).

[9]Peter Woll, *American Bureaucracy*, 2d ed. (New York: W. W. Norton, 1977), p. 194.

[10]Werner Hirsch, *Urban Economic Analysis* (New York: McGraw-Hill, 1973).

[11]Robert J. Staaf, "The Public School System in Transition: Consolidation and Parental Choice," *Budgets and Bureaucrats: The Sources of Government Growth*, ed. Thomas Borcherding (Durham, N.C.: Duke University Press, 1977), pp. 130–47.

36

4

PUBLIC VERSUS PRIVATE PROVISION OF GOODS AND SERVICES: THE EVIDENCE

There have been many investigations into the relative efficiency of the private vis-à-vis the public sector in providing such services as refuse collection, fire protection, debt collection, health care and hospitals, ship repair, electric utilities, and airline services. Less comprehensive, but useful, studies have also been made of weather· forecasting, policing services, ambulance service, and education. Some of these activities are, or have been, regulated by government, including airlines, utilities, and hospitals. Moreover, health facilities are also often regulated through the accreditation process by private associations. Regulation, especially that which guarantees a specific level of profits, reduces the incentives for cutting costs and may also inhibit a company from achieving an efficient scale of operations. For example, airline routes were previously allocated and utilities are required to provide service to all users in their service area. Yet the private sector, despite such restrictions, has been found so consistently more efficient that economist Thomas Borcherding has suggested the "Bureaucratic Rule of Two: Removal of an activity from the private to the public sector will double its unit costs of production."[1] The Bureaucratic Rule of Two holds that the taxpayers can have the same services at half the cost. This is a very important conclusion, especially when it is realized that some of the studies did not even take into account all of the costs of government provision of goods and services. If these costs had been taken into account, transferring public services to the private sector would show even greater savings to the taxpayer.

The True Cost of Publicly Provided Services

Almost all studies of public-private cost comparisons are biased in favor of the public sector, because the figures for the public sector seldom include all of the costs that should properly be charged to the various services. Bureaucrats have a strong incentive to expand the size of government, so it is in their best interest to make the costs of providing services to the taxpayer seem as reasonable as possible. Public hearings held by the Small Business Administration provide many examples of public employee deception regarding the true costs of government services.[2] Most often overlooked are what economists call "opportunity costs," plus pension liabilities, taxes, and license fees.

Opportunity Costs. Opportunity costs are defined as the benefit forgone, or opportunity lost, when any resource (such as land, labor, or capital) is used in one way instead of in its next best alternative use.[3] For example, the opportunity costs when government creates a recreational park might be the benefits lost by the public had the land been zoned as an industrial park to attract private industry. These firms would produce consumer goods and services in addition to paying property and other taxes that could be used to reduce the general tax burden. If there is high employment in the economy and the government decides to provide a large number of goods and services, the opportunity costs are the benefits gained from consumer and capital goods that would have been privately produced instead. In a fully employed economy, the opportunity cost of every one dollar the government spends is one dollar less output in the private economy.

For the private firm, failure to consider opportunity costs reduces profits, and therefore threatens the long-run survival of the organization. If a private businessman were to ignore the fact that his capital assets could earn larger profits if he used them to produce, say, soybeans rather than cotton, he would not survive long in the competitive marketplace. However, government is in many cases a monopoly supplier of goods and services and does not have to compete in the marketplace. As long as taxpayers can be persuaded that certain services should be financed and provided by the government, there is no danger of a public firm going out of business. When both the public and private sectors compete in providing the same service, the self-inter-

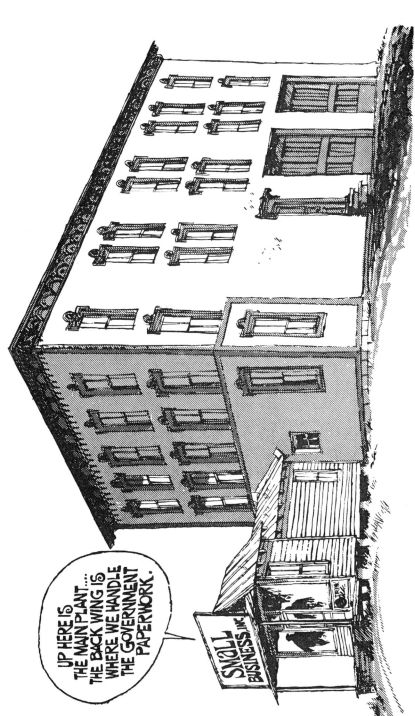

ested bureaucrat has a strong incentive to underreport costs in order to gain the favor of the taxpayers who support the service. It is not surprising, then, that opportunity costs are so often overlooked in the public sector.

Pension Liabilities. Federal, state, and municipal government pensions represent an enormous financial burden on U.S. taxpayers. Pension benefits being given to government employees are now growing much faster than the funds appropriated to pay for them. Therefore, the gap between total pension obligations and the actual dollars available to pay for them (unfunded liabilities) has widened alarmingly. There are, in fact, many local governments that do not set aside any funds at all to finance pensions but operate on a pay-as-you-go basis. If the budget is increased to reduce unfunded liabilities, taxpayers might refuse to bear the huge burden.

There are about 2,100 state and city pension plans in the U.S. and 200 established on a county basis. These plans cover around 9.5 million public employees and the vast majority of the contributions to these plans are paid by the governments rather than employees.[4]

Financial problems resulting from pension costs have become severe for many northeastern and midwestern cities. These regions have become early problem areas because of declines in city population. The most notorious case is New York City, which tripled its pension payments during the past ten years. According to a study conducted by Sen. Thomas Eagleton, New York City spends $1.2 billion annually on pensions but should be spending an additional $700 million per year to finance the fund adequately.[5] By 1985 New York City will have acquired $3 billion in unfunded pension liabilities. Washington, D.C., already has unfunded liabilities exceeding $1 billion and currently makes no contributions to the police and fire pension plans. The police and fire pension fund in Los Angeles has unfunded liabilities of more than $1.2 billion. Recently, Detroit was forced by a court decision to levy a special property tax assessment to provide $18 million in additional funding for the city's bus drivers' pension.[6]

In a review of 72 state and local government pension plans the General Accounting Office (GAO) found that 53 of them were funded below the level required by the federal government of private firms! State and local jurisdictions had simply pushed pension costs into the future for someone else to pay. Now the day of reckoning has arrived.

40

A typical city is Hamtramck, Michigan, with a population of 26,000. Pension increases were enormous although, at the same time, funding was practically nonexistent. Such fiscal irresponsibility has forced 99 percent of the city's property tax receipts to be funneled into the police and fire pension funds to keep them afloat. Unless taxes are increased, Hamtramck public employees' pension payments will be halted next year. As an illustration of how insane the public pension system has become, one Hamtramck employee contributed only $35 to his retirement plan while working, but has collected over a quarter of a million dollars in benefits since his retirement![7]

Because pension obligations can be deferred, a city may avoid paying for some or even all of the accruing benefits until an employee retires. Therefore, people who may have had no part in the decision to grant large pension benefits ultimately end up paying for the policies of earlier administrations. Citizens face catastrophic increases in taxes when public employees who were granted huge pension benefits reach retirement age.

In addition, the failure to recognize pyramiding pension costs may distort the overall public employee compensation decision. In other words, bigger pensions can be offered if they don't have to be paid immediately. Both bureaucrats and politicians may push for larger pensions instead of higher paychecks so current taxes will not have to be increased very much. Department of Commerce statistics show that spending for employee retirement programs during 1962–72 increased much faster than spending for total payroll outlays.[8] Brookings Institution scholars Harry Wellington and Ralph Winter have noted that

> Where pensions are concerned, moreover, major concessions may be politically tempting since there is no immediate impact on the taxpayer or the city budget. Whereas actuarial soundness would be insisted on by a profit-seeking entity like a firm, it may be a secondary concern to politicians whose conduct is determined by relatively short-run considerations. The impact of failing to adhere to actuarial principles will frequently fall upon a different mayor and a different city council. In those circumstances, concessions that condemn a city to future impoverishment may not seem intolerable.[9]

Probably the most extreme example of this fiscal irresponsibility involves New York City. The trustees of New York City pension plans failed for as long as 50 years to revise false actuarial assumptions. As a consequence, when New York finally got around to recomputing pension liabilities with realistic figures, the city discovered that funding of the pension for fiscal year 1976 would have to be increased by about $460 million, or 38 percent, if contributions were to continue at the same rate.[10]

At the federal level, funding deficiencies for social security and federal employee pension funds are appalling. In 1977 expected future payments for social security, civil service pensions, and retirement pay for military personnel exceeded anticipated contributions by the outrageous sum of $5 trillion, representing an average annual growth of 39.2 percent. Pension liabilities at the federal level have doubled, on average, about every two years.[11] Such a rate of growth cannot long be sustained without either huge increases in taxes or benefit payment reductions.

Taxes and License Fees. Government agencies that provide goods and services to the public don't have to pay taxes and license fees. The private firm, however, is swamped by tax payments to federal, state, and local governments. Private-firm revenues are eaten away by income taxes and social-security contributions to the federal government, sales taxes and unemployment contributions to state government, and property taxes to local government. License fees are assessed primarily at the state and local levels and include such charges as occupational licenses (or corporate charters) and automobile license plates. Other examples of governmental assessments, which private firms pay but competing public agencies do not, are vehicle inspection fees and gasoline taxes (road-use tax).

Because government agencies don't have to pay taxes and license fees, bookkeepers simply exclude such items from the public-sector cost calculations. However, the exemption of government agencies from payment of taxes and license fees does not mean that these costs are not incurred. Public-sector vehicle repair and inspection and highway maintenance must be paid for by someone. Whether government service agencies pay these costs from their individual budgets or not, they are still financed by citizen taxpayers. In other words, the general public bears the cost of government-provided goods and services regardless of who counts these costs.

42

It is also true that taxes and license fees represent opportunity costs to government. For example, the decision to have refuse collection in New York City provided by the city government has cost the city millions of dollars in tax revenue and license fees, which would have been collected if trash collection had been provided by private firms. Instead, New York bureaucrats chose to monopolize trash collection and finance the service out of both user charges and increased tax collections.

Regulatory Costs. One of the most dramatic examples of regulatory inequity is found in the electric utilities industry. The Tennessee Valley Authority (TVA), which is a government producer of electricity, is the country's largest sulfur dioxide polluter, accounting for 38 percent of total sulfur emissions in the Southeast. This agency's compliance record with EPA (Environmental Protection Agency) pollution laws is disgraceful. As of 1977 only 16 percent of TVA electric power facilities were in compliance with EPA pollution standards, whereas 74 percent of the privately owned electric utilities were in compliance with the law. The Department of Defense provides another example of regulatory immunity. DOD discharges over 335 million gallons of human waste per day yet only 30 percent of this waste receives secondary pollution treatment or less.[12]

Astonishingly, many economists who have researched the costs of public versus private provision of goods and services have also adopted the Bureaucratic Rule of Two when there are so many important costs of doing business that are simply ignored by government agencies. Maybe they should apply a bureaucratic rule of four.

Cost Comparisons Between the Public and Private Sectors

Refuse Collection. Refuse collection is of particular interest for three reasons. First, this technologically simple activity, which is carried out at the local level of government and by private firms as well, illustrates many of the problems associated with making public-private cost comparisons. Second, in contrast to firms that are regulated or limited to a given service area or route, private garbage firms may adjust to their most efficient size of operation. Third, in the absence

43

of government restrictions, trash collection in the private sector should be fiercely competitive and pressures for cost minimization especially intense; large amounts of capital equipment are not required, nor are there any other real economic barriers to entry. Refuse collection should clearly show the superiority of the private sector, but the evidence may, at first glance, seem conflicting. That is because some of the researchers excluded important costs or made faulty assumptions. When all costs are taken into account, and the correct approach taken in making the public-private comparison, the private sector is shown to be far less expensive.

The first case study of refuse collection was conducted by UCLA economist Werner Hirsch, who found that there did not appear to be any major differences between public and private costs of residential refuse collection.[13] In contrast, data from Monmouth County, New Jersey, showed that the average cost per person of trash collection was 70 percent higher when services were provided by the government.[14] A Connecticut study concluded that refuse collection costs appeared to vary with the type of economic environment in which collection was provided: private collection appeared to be about 30 percent more expensive than municipal collection, which, in turn, appeared to be about 25 percent more expensive than contract collection.[15] These Connecticut results were supported by a study conducted by the Columbia University School of Business, which found that market competition in garbage collection is from 26 percent to 48 percent more expensive than single-contractor arrangements.[16] The Columbia University study looked at 340 different public and private refuse collection firms operating in an equal number of cities. Recent research undertaken in Canada reported, however, that private-sector collection of garbage is far less costly than municipal collection in 48 Canadian communities, each with populations exceeding 10,000.[17] So the evidence seems to be conflicting.

Clearly, an explanation is needed. A major weakness of all previous studies of private versus public cost of garbage collection is that virtually all failed to recognize that each municipality might use different accounting practices. Instead of taking this into account, earlier studies simply assumed that cost accounting methods were the same in all communities and that budget items represented identical types of operating costs. As is well known, there is little comparability among budgeting practices of different cities. Most local governments allocate a lump-sum budget to agencies and allow bureau managers to dole out funds as they see fit. Unfortunately, as pointed out in Chapter 3, large amounts of money usually end up as perquisites. Also, an individual municipality may not even be aware of the true cost of publicly provided services. Even though some local governments might maintain a separate budget and expenditure account for trash collection, figures hardly ever include all of the costs that should be charged.[18] Therefore, most studies comparing different municipalities with private firms are biased in favor of the municipality. Biases of this sort can be great; figures for refuse collection in Hartford, Connecticut, underestimated the actual cost by 41 percent, because the costs of vehicle operation and maintenance, interest, and depreciation were not included.[19] Further, the concept of opportunity cost is virtually unknown in government bureaucracy. Uncollected property tax revenues resulting from municipal operation (which underestimates the true cost of municipal collection) were estimated to be an additional 2.3 percent of Hartford's budget for trash removal.[20] None of the previous studies considered the future cost of pension payments of retiring municipal employees! Obviously, leaving out such important costs makes municipal collection look like a bargain compared to private collection.

But suppose we compare the prices charged by private firms in a single governmental jurisdiction with those charged by the same municipality for public collection. Such cases, fortunately, are not rare. The authors have analyzed trash service charges for some Virginia suburbs of Washington, D.C., where 29 private firms serve almost the same geographical areas as the public enterprise. Cost figures showed, after adjustment for frequency of service and for income tax deduction benefits to homeowners, that public service was about twice as costly as private refuse collection—the rule of two.[21]

Fairfax County's Solid Waste Division of Public Works collects trash once each week at approximately one-third of the single-family homes in the county. All homeowners pay a flat fee of $86.00 per year plus $0.06 per $100 of the assessed value of the property for leaf collection—whether or not the property owner enjoys the luxury of trees or disposes of leaves via the county service. According to the tax assessor's office, the average value of a single-family dwelling in the county is $68,000. So the typical family pays a total of $126.80 for public refuse services, including $40.80 for leaf collection. The Solid Waste Division asserts that the fees collected cover all costs of collection except for unfunded retirement benefits, which are paid from general revenues. Equipment, maintenance, and operating expenditures are charged to the Solid Waste Division of Public Works. The public service, like private firms, is charged $7.60 per ton for dumping by the county public landfill authority.

Those homes in the county not served by the public trash collection agency must contract individually with one of the 29 private firms in the area. Not all firms serve all areas, but competition is intense. At least five companies compete in each of the residential neighborhoods where the authors reside. Of the 29 private firms only one firm charged as much as Fairfax County. For the 29 firms surveyed, the average charge was $85.76 per year.

Much stronger conclusions can be drawn when the quality of service is taken into account. Virtually all private firms surveyed provided collection twice weekly, double that of public service. Both public and private operations require homeowners to place garbage in containers at the curb, although a number of private companies offer the option of behind-the-house pickup at somewhat higher fees. When the frequency of refuse collection is considered, the cost of public collection becomes four times as great as for private collection. Private firms offer twice as much service at half the cost!

In addition, the private firms must meet costs that the public enterprise does not, and yet all charge their customers much lower fees. The government enterprise is exempt from all taxes (including federal, state, and local income and gasoline taxes), license fees, and bonding requirements. Moreover, the private companies are presumably operating to make a profit or at least break even. Therefore, prices are set at a level that will allow private firms to cover at least their costs.

The bureaucratic disincentives discussed in Chapter 3 make it practically impossible for publicly provided services such as refuse collection to be offered efficiently and at low costs. Absenteeism rates are far higher among employees of municipal agencies than among those employed by private firms. Public employees who work in trash collection agencies are absent 12 percent of the time while the employees of private firms are away from the job only 7.5 percent of working days. Municipal departments also use larger pickup crews, averaging 3.26 persons as opposed to 2.18 for private companies. These larger municipal crews serve fewer households per shift (632 families as against 686 families) and spend more time servicing each household per year (4.35 man-hours for public agencies, 2.37 man-hours for private firms). Further, municipal agencies tend to use smaller trucks, which cause them to make more frequent trips to the dump site. Average capacity for municipal trucks is 19.8 cubic yards, and 23.1 cubic yards for private trucks.[22]

The National Center on Productivity has reported that the majority of city-run trash collection routes are inefficiently designed. This causes costly waste of man-hours and fuel, and leads to increased maintenance costs. Poor routing usually results from the failure to keep down travel time from the area served and the disposal site. Private-sector firms must follow efficient routes if they are to survive in the marketplace; therefore, the private sector naturally has incentives for efficient route design. The public enterprise has little motivation to be efficient since salaries are paid from tax revenues in addition to user charges.

The National Productivity Center also showed that a large number of cities retain huge fleets of collection vehicles that are not adequately serviced and maintained. Many cities select poor-quality collection equipment and keep vehicles in service much longer than required. New York City's Sanitation Department was so incompetently managed that 36 percent of its trash collection trucks were in the shop during 1969.[23]

Fire Protection. Fire protection is a public service generally provided by municipal governments through volunteers or paid employees. However, communities such as Scottsdale, Arizona; Grant's Pass, Oregon; and Billings, Montana, contract for this service with a private firm. In Scottsdale, fire protection became a private service when former journalist Lou Witzeman moved into the area in 1947. At that time, Scottsdale was not incorporated and was thus without public services. So Witzeman collected $10 per year from a thousand residents and started the Rural/Metro Fire Protection Company, Inc., with a single fire engine. As a profit-oriented firm, Rural/Metro has had to use efficient cost-cutting equipment and techniques to keep Scottsdale residents' business.

Employees construct the firm's equipment. The equipment built in-

47

house lacks the fancy chrome so typical of the traditional fire engine. Accessories can add thousands of dollars to costs, but add nothing to firefighting ability. Witzeman's firm has managed to keep costs down by adapting existing fire engines designed for use on desert brush fires. These smaller vehicles were faster, and although they had a lower water capacity (300 gallons), were able to handle 75 percent of all fires.[24] One of the most interesting technological innovations of the Scottsdale firm is a remote-control firefighting device. This battery-powered piece of equipment is mounted on tractor treads and is able to maneuver several hundred feet with a swivel hose nozzle. Because this machine can resist temperatures up to 700 degrees Fahrenheit, it can be used to control fires in areas men cannot go. Small inexpensive two-man trucks have been used by Rural/Metro to replace some conventional engines. In many communities, small fires, such as trash fires, cause a large number of alarms. These calls are easily handled, in Scottsdale, by the two-man pickup truck, which has been altered to carry a water tank and pump. These smaller "attack trucks" offer a tremendous economic advantage in that they cost only $6,000 (vs. $60,000 for a conventional fire truck) and require fewer firefighters.[25]

Rural/Metro is also a licensed fire equipment producer and can build water pumpers with a 1,000 gallon per minute capacity at a cost of $30,000, which is about one-half the cost of a standard pumper of equal capacity. Further, the Scottsdale firm has designed and constructed a dual pumper that can be mounted on a forklift on the tailgate of a fire engine and can be connected to one water hydrant while the main engine pump is attached to another hydrant, providing the equivalent of two pumpers on one truck. The cost of such a device is about the same as the price of a conventional single-pump engine.[26] In addition, Rural/Metro acquired four-inch German fire hoses as opposed to the standard 2.5-inch hose used by most American municipal services. This has allowed the firm to put out larger fires with fewer employees. Finally, Witzeman's firm was one of the first fire protection services to paint fire engines lime-yellow, rather than red, to make them more visible day and night. The result has been a three-quarter reduction in the number of rear-end collisions.

If Scottsdale's fire protection service were to be provided by municipal government it would cost $7.10 per person.[27] The Rural/Metro Company, however, was paid $3.78 per person, a cost saving of $3.32

or approximately 47 percent.[28] Therefore, if the public sector were to provide the fire protection instead of the private sector, per capita costs could be expected to double, another example of the Bureaucratic Rule of Two.

Since Rural/Metro Company's service was contracted for by the city of Scottsdale, the after-tax profit rate of the firm was regulated not to exceed seven percent of gross revenue. This regulation might be expected to eliminate incentives to reduce costs, but this is not the case, for

> there is an incentive for the company to minimize costs. Growth is predicated upon being able to maintain current customers and develop new sources of business. If costs are not kept in check, newly formed communities will not have an incentive to purchase the service and existing customers may seek alternative sources of supply. Potential competition exists in the form of the threat of the municipality producing its own service or contracting with another producer.[29]

Also, the fire insurance rating for Scottsdale is no different from that of other comparable cities, which indicates that, although the cost of provision of fire services in Scottsdale is a lot lower, the quality of service is as good or better.

The success of Rural/Metro in Scottsdale has led to a demand for the firm's services in 13 other Arizona communities and one community in Tennessee. Another private firm, Wackenhut Corporation, has operated a 150-employee fire protection service for the Kennedy Space Flight Center at Cape Canaveral, Florida. Without doubt, all communities could benefit from contracting fire protection services with private firms. However, since labor-related expenses make up about 90 percent of municipal fire department expenditures, such measures will meet with extreme resistance from bureaucratic empire builders and public employee unions. If citizens desire to reduce taxes, they must challenge the power of these interest groups.

The Rural/Metro Company operates two-man engines, mentioned above, and supplements these squads with paid reservists when needed. This technique, known as the Scottsdale Plan, minimizes the number of full-time employees drawing salaries and fringe benefits while spending much of their time waiting for fires to occur. Reservists are placed on retainer and also receive an hourly rate during training and firefighting. They are usually on call one week every month.[30]

Another drawback to public provision of such services as refuse collection, fire protection, and police and security services is that the public agency is the sole source of supply. When public employees strike, essential public services are withdrawn and no alternatives are available. Consider the disruptions caused by the recent strikes of firefighters in Kansas City and Chicago; public employee unions are becoming more aggressive and the result is usually higher taxes to pay for increased wages. If trash collection services were provided by competing firms, a homeowner who was inconvenienced when one firm went on strike could easily switch to a competitor. The threat of losing business to rivals would reduce the likelihood of strikes, slow-downs, "sick-ins," and similar disruptions.

Debt Collection. The federal government is not only the nation's largest debtor, but also its largest creditor. The General Accounting Office has reported that $118 billion was owed the federal government as of 1979.[31] In addition to the huge total of uncollected debt, the amount of defaulted loans is growing rapidly. The sums due the government increased by $15 billion, or 21 percent, during 1977. Far more than the private sector, the federal government is plagued by nonpayment of loans; the disastrous student-loan program was one of the primary causes of this financial mess. The Treasury Department says that government write-offs of bad debts totaled $13 billion at the end of 1976, an increase of 35 percent over the previous year.[32] Unlike the private sector, the government takes a very apathetic attitude toward debt collection. An audit by the comptroller general of the U.S. found that only three government agencies out of 12 had ever established allowances for uncollectible debts. Most agencies simply wrote off accounts and made no attempt to collect them. Many debts are incurred through bureau errors in making overpayments. As of 1978 the Social Security Administration had made excessive payments totaling $1.5 billion.[33] No wonder the debts go uncollected. If agencies attempted to recover these losses, bureaucratic errors of gross overpayment would be exposed.

The Treasury Department makes double payments on more than

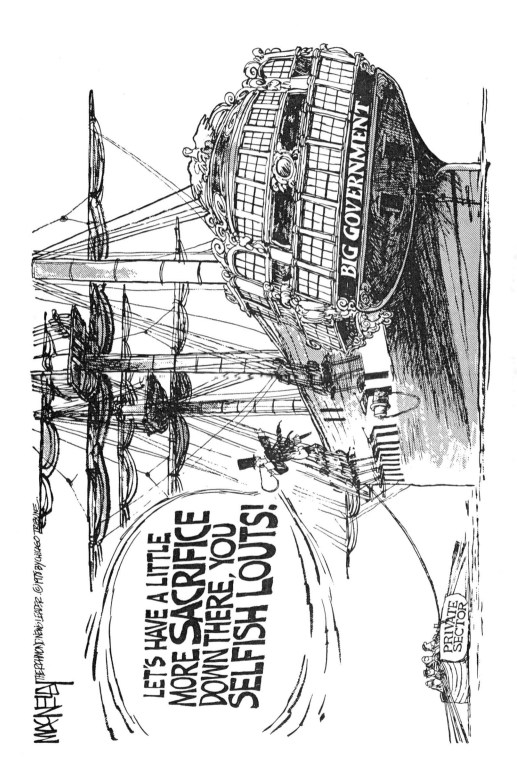

100,000 government checks a year and has made no attempt whatever to recover the $73 million in overpayments made over three years. Such double payments are usually made when recipients report that their checks were lost. Without questioning these inquiries, the Treasury immediately issues a replacement check and does not stop payment on the original check. The original check is quite often illegally cashed by either the recipient or a check forger. A Secret Service investigation discovered that the Treasury failed to take any steps to recover the money lost this way. Of the $86 million worth of backlogged cases, almost all of them represent double payments made since 1976. In its report, the Secret Service charged that the buildup of overpayment accounts was due to the failure of the Treasury Department management to deal with the problem and to a lack of efficient procedures to handle double payments. The Treasury Department is responsible for issuing 600 million of the 700 million government checks processed each year. The average amount of each double-payment check is about $200, according to the Secret Service.[34]

The tremendous backlog of reissued checks was uncovered when Secret Service personnel noticed a sudden decline in the number of cases that were referred for investigation. Employees of the Treasury Department explained that managers had deliberately hidden double-payment cases among backlogged accounts. Agents discovered cases dating back to 1970 that should have been routinely processed. The Secret Service reported that it received complaints stating that "the Treasury operation was mismanaged, did not stand up to banks that refused to cooperate in efforts to track down fraud, and did not have accurate statistics on its operation."[35] In its study of debt collection, the General Accounting Office declared that federal "collection methods are expensive and slow compared with commercial practices and are not cost-effective in dealing with debtors who delay or try to avoid paying."[36] Generally, the government does not seek judgment on debts of less than $600. Commercial firms say that it is economical to pursue collection to the point of court judgment for claims as small as $25. The GAO found that one large agency spent an average of $8.72 to collect debts, but that comparable costs for a commercial firm were less than $3.50 for the same operations.[37]

In the private sector, court judgments are normally sought within five months, but the federal government takes a year, and frequently much longer. Therefore, by the federal government's own assessment, debt collection, when undertaken at all, is far less efficient than its private counterpart. Government bad debts increase the tax burden and the federal deficit, yet agencies are now barred from using private collection agencies, except when given explicit legislative authority.

Ship Repair. Naval support ships are, in many ways, similar to private merchant marine vessels. In fact, naval fleet supply oilers, which refuel U.S. Navy ships at sea, are much like merchant tankers. Between 1971 and 1977, commercial tankers under contract with the federal government actually conducted more than 90 at-sea refueling operations for the Military Sealift Command.[38] There are, however, considerable differences between commercial and naval ships in the amount of time spent at sea and in the cost of maintenance. Naval support ships are on sea duty only about 20 percent of the time. Comparable commercial ships are at sea between 40 and 70 percent of the time. Because the wear and tear on equipment is greatest when a ship is at sea, you would expect commercial vessels to have maintenance costs far greater than those of naval ships. That's not the case. The GAO found that the navy's maintenance costs per ship average

Table 6

Comparison of Selected Maintenance and Repair Costs for Similar Equipment Items on Navy Oilers and Commercial Tankers

Equipment Item	Naval Oilers	Commercial Tankers	Naval Commercial
Boiler refractory	$40,270.50	$2,860.50	14:1
Pumps, main feed	32,035.00	618.00	51:8
Pumps, cargo	80,380.80	3,328.00	24:2
Pumps, fire and flush	25,921.60	1,221.00	21:2
Propeller shaft, bearings	36,829.60	2,745.00	13:4
Turbines, nonengine	20,823.00	6,349.00	3:3
Turbines, service generator	66,111.20	4,044.00	16:3
Valves, safety	3,620.00	288.00	12:6

SOURCE: U.S. General Accounting Office, *The Navy Overhaul Policy—A Costly Means of Insuring Readiness for Support Ships,* Report by Comptroller General of the United States: LCD-78-434, December 27, 1978, p. 42.

53

about $2 million a year, compared with about $400,000 a year for a similar commercial ship. Both naval and commercial repair and maintenance costs for similar items of equipment are shown in Table 6. The third column in the table represents the ratio of the costs of naval ship maintenance and repair to commercial tanker maintenance and repair costs.

It is clear—maintenance costs for naval ships exceed those of similar commercial ships by, at the very least, three times and at the most about 52 times.

In addition, the typical naval support ship spends between 30 and 68 days in repair each year. A comparable commercial ship is out of service for only 11 to 31 days a year. This finding is particularly surprising, for a naval ship is of little, if any, strategic value while in port. One would think that the ability to repair and maintain ship equipment while at sea would be a top priority in U.S. naval operations. Strangely, the opposite is true. Commercial ships make as many repairs as possible while under way and naval vessels usually make repairs while in port. Such a result is especially dramatic since commercial ships carry a crew of only a fraction of the size of the crew on naval ships. GAO found that the *largest* crew size employed among the commercial ships it studied was 46, whereas the *smallest* crew size among naval support ships was 92. Of the 58 naval support ships examined by GAO, crew size ranged as high as 1,438 with an average of 555.[39] The General Accounting Office concluded that the navy could reduce maintenance costs dramatically without significantly affecting the readiness of the fleet by adopting commercial maintenance practices.

Some years ago, it might be noted, naval shipyards ceased construction of new naval ships and all new construction was contracted out to private yards, because construction costs were much lower at private facilities under competitively bid contracts.

Electric Utilities. The electric utilities industry is unique because all private-sector electric utilities are regulated by government. By far, the most common form of regulation is rate-of-return or cost-plus regulation. Electric utilities are allowed to receive a fixed percentage rate of return above all legitimate costs. Regulation of this type reduces the incentives for efficiency because firms cannot necessarily increase their profit margin by cutting costs. However, electric utility firms still have some incentives to lower costs since there is no guarantee that, in periods of rapidly rising costs, electricity rate increases will be approved fast enough to keep up with inflation; utility rate hearings are notoriously slow.

A recent study conducted by the General Accounting Office showed that if federal government hydroelectric plants were as efficient as comparable plants in the private sector, annual operating and maintenance costs of the federal plants would be about $11.7 million less.[40] The GAO examined 95 government plants and 47 private-sector plants. The cost of producing electricity among private electric power plants averaged $2.72 per kilowatt-hour while federal plants averaged $3.29 per kilowatt-hour.[41]

Federal hydroelectric plants have been criticized for employing too many workers. During the period 1973–75, federal power plants had about 48 percent more employees per plant than private utilities. If government power plants had operated with the same number of employees, they would have needed 447 fewer workers. If we assume that each employee received a $20,000 annual salary (the average salary for federal employees in 1977), the additional cost amounts to $8.9 million a year.[42]

GAO also found that public hydroelectric plants were much less progressive than private plants in adopting technological improvements to reduce production costs. Delays in the design or installation of automated production techniques, such as remote-control equipment, have prevented the federal government from saving about $1.5 million each year in the 17 plants surveyed.[43]

Airline Services. In the United States, airline services are provided exclusively by the private sector so that no direct comparison can be made between private firms and public firms. However, until recently, private airlines were strictly regulated by the Civil Aeronautics Board (CAB) and profit incentives were reduced. During 1978 CAB, under the direction of Alfred Kahn, deregulated airline fares and route controls so that most of the incentives of profit-seeking firms were restored to the air-travel industry. Before airline deregulation, that industry was more like a public-sector service than a profit-oriented private enterprise. Government control over the prices of airline tickets and the areas where airlines were allowed to fly virtually eliminated incentives for efficiency and caused industry managers to become more bureaucratic. The changes brought about by airline deregulation give us an opportunity to make a sharp comparison.

As a result of deregulation, regularly scheduled airlines have instituted new flights in over 100 cities, and 231 completely new routes have been added by as many as 35 commercial carriers. The increased competition has dramatically reduced air fares. Since deregulation, of course, fares have risen because of skyrocketing fuel prices. Still, about 50 percent of all commercial airline customers now receive price discounts on air travel. Discount fares and increased service to Florida resulted in an increase in passenger demand at Miami Airport by 21 percent. Air traffic in general was up by 13.5 percent for the first nine months of 1979 and an increase of 17 percent was reported during 1978.[44]

Airline services in Australia are provided by both a private carrier, Ansett Airline, and a public carrier, Trans Australian Airlines (TAA). Both airlines are strictly controlled by government. Government control is so thorough that the two airline fleets in any given year will have exactly the same number and models of airplanes. All main routes are the same for both airlines and the departure and arrival times are identical. Ansett and Trans Australian planes provide the same services and foods. The wages paid by both airlines are the same. Also, each airline carries approximately the same quantity of mail. Amazingly, even the separate restaurants maintained by the two airlines have the same number of tables and chairs.[45] Because practically all physical characteristics of Ansett and TAA have been regulated to the point that they are virtually identical, differences in performance can arise only from management incentives.

In Table 7, three efficiency measures are reported for the period 1958–59 to 1973–74. The private airline outperformed its public counterpart in every year regardless of the efficiency measure considered. The Bureaucratic Rule of Two appears to apply only to the tons of freight and mail carried per employee. But given the extreme regulation to which the private carrier was subjected, it is surprising that there are any differences at all. For example, when TAA purchased a new airplane, Ansett was required by the Australian government to buy the very same make and model. The government also attempted to prevent any competitive gains by requiring all new planes to be introduced into service at both the same day and hour.[46] The fact that the private firm,

Table 7

Three Measures of Efficiency for
Public and Private Airlines in Australia
1958–59 to 1973–74

Year	Tons of Freight & Mail Carried Per Employee			Passengers Carried Per Employee			Revenue Earned Per Employee		
	Ansett*	TAA**	Ratio	Ansett*	TAA**	Ratio	Ansett*	TAA**	Ratio
1958–59	10.69	4.42	2:42	282	217	1:30	$ 7,172	$ 6,104	1:17
1959–60	10.77	4.57	2:36	309	259	1:19	7,758	7,016	1:11
1960–61	10.96	4.52	2:42	337	228	1:48	8,679	7,052	1:23
1961–62	10.84	4.64	2:34	331	246	1:35	8,425	7,367	1:14
1962–63	11.09	4.69	2:36	316	255	1:24	8,510	7,726	1:10
1963–64	11.06	4.83	2:29	324	274	1:18	9,071	8,093	1:12
1964–65	12.14	5.02	2:42	352	287	1:23	9,705	8,553	1:13
1965–66	11.08	4.88	2:27	354	294	1:20	10,479	9,072	1:16
1966–67	10.34	5.11	2:02	348	316	1:10	10,829	9,954	1:09
1967–68	9.57	5.41	1:77	363	337	1:08	12,080	11,033	1:09
1968–69	9.54	5.34	1:79	392	356	1:10	13,185	11,734	1:12
1969–70	9.35	5.80	1:61	414	390	1:06	14,118	13,146	1:07
1970–71	8.75	5.70	1:54	417	399	1:05	15,558	14,522	1:10
1971–72	8.82	5.63	1:57	437	414	1:06	17,280	15,644	1:10
1972–73	9.07	5.62	1:61	468	449	1:04	17,829	16,541	1:08
1973–74	10.02	6.06	1:65	532	496	1:07	21,461	19,183	1:12
Average	10.25	5.14	2:03	373	326	1:17	12,009	10,740	1:12

SOURCE: David G. Davies, ''Property Rights and Economic Efficiency—The Australian Airlines Revisited,'' *Journal of Law and Economics* 20 (April 1977) p. 226.

*Private airline.
**Public Airline.

Ansett, was able to outperform the public firm, TAA, consistently over 16 years is impressive testimony to the powerful incentives that exist in the private relative to the public sector.

Weather Forecasting. For years, a six-member weather observation team has been maintained at Washington, D.C., National Airport by the National Weather Service, a part of the U.S. Department of Commerce. In 1978 the annual cost of this operation was $237,000. In July 1979 the operation was contracted to a private firm that had underbid 27 other firms with a low bid of $67,000 per year. Even when government overhead costs are included and the salaries of two federal employees who remained on the job are taken into account, the total annual costs are only $152,000—a saving of $85,000 obtained by merely shifting four jobs from the public to the private sector.[47]

In addition, the private firm has an incentive for forecasting accuracy. The National Weather Service "grades" forecasts on a monthly basis. If the forecasts are inadequate two months in succession, the contract can be judged in default.

Ambulance Service. Hundreds of cities provide emergency ambulance service along with publicly provided police or fire departments. Yet there is no reason for governments to be offering such services. Private organizations have demonstrated that reliable ambulance service can be provided at lower costs.

The Bethesda–Chevy Chase Rescue Squad, Inc., located in the Washington, D.C., area, is an example. This nonprofit corporation is staffed entirely by volunteers. Funding comes primarily from fund-raising drives, donations, and interest income. The rescue squad is equipped to handle paramedic-type duties in addition to its normal ambulance-rescue operations. Equipment includes six paramedic vans, three ambulances, a mobile intensive care unit, a crash truck, and a rescue boat. During 1974 the rescue squad answered more than 8,000 calls for ambulance, rescue, and paramedic services. The organization provides the services mentioned with an annual operating budget of only $220,000, or $27.50 per call. Local taxpayers save millions of dollars. More than 150 volunteers belong to the rescue squad; if these squad members were maintained on a local government payroll it would cost taxpayers about $3 million, not to mention operation and maintenance costs.[48]

Some critics of private ambulance services admit that private firms might effectively compete with government operations in densely populated areas such as Washington, D.C. However, they state that government must intervene to meet the needs of rural areas. They haven't heard about the Acadian Ambulance Service, Inc. It successfully serves around 500,000 rural residents of Louisiana's 6,000-square-mile Acadian region. This profit-seeking firm maintains 24 ambulances at 13 substations and handles more than 60 calls per day. The company does not receive state, local, or federal government support. Its revenue comes from a $15 annual subscription fee paid by 74,000 families. Although the service is available to all residents of the Acadian region of Louisiana, subscribing members receive free emergency transportation and reduced rates on routine patient transfers.[49]

Policing Services. One of the largest items in any municipal police department budget is the cost of personnel. Therefore, most tax savings gained from more efficient police services must come by reducing the size of police forces without sacrificing quality of service. In Fort Lauderdale, Florida, civilians were hired to investigate traffic accidents and enforce vehicle regulations. The state legislature of Florida has empowered 16 civilian traffic safety aides to issue traffic citations. Contracting out to private individuals has relieved regular police officers of 75 percent of the traffic-associated work and allowed them to devote more time to criminal activity.[50]

In Scottsdale, Arizona, the local government has adopted a program in which authorized civilians handle all noncrime calls for assistance. The civilian personnel were required to meet the same entry requirements as regular police officers but received only about half the normal training. This arrangement saved Scottsdale taxpayers about $26,000 annually.

An alternative to the traditional municipal police department is suggested by the private security industry. Although most of the security industry's functions consist of guard, alarm, and investigation services, many firms can do everything that public-sector police departments do. In most cases, employees of private security companies have only citizen's arrest authority, which allows them legally to respond to noncriminal calls, do traffic duty, patrolling, and investigation. The major difference between the typical security officer and a government police officer is simply the broader arrest authority of the latter. To avoid restrictions on arrest powers, several private security firms have enrolled their security officers in certified police academies where, upon graduation, they become qualified as fully empowered police officers. Thoroughly trained personnel are currently used by some private firms to provide complete police service to small communities. Buffalo Creek, West Virginia, contracts with Guardsmark, Inc., a security firm in Memphis, Tennessee, for all its police services. In addition, Guardsmark has negotiated with Del Mar, California, to provide complete police services.

The Wackenhut Corporation serves several communities in the state of Florida. Indian River, Florida, has contracted with Wackenhut for complete service for the past five years. Wackenhut also acts as the entire police department for the U.S. Department of Energy's 1,600-square-mile Mercury Test Site in Nevada.[51]

Education. By far, the largest item in educational budgets is salaries. As pointed out in Chapter 3, there are positive incentives for public-sector managers to inflate the number of employees under their supervision in order to receive promotions and increases in income. Therefore, one might expect that any cost comparisons between public and private education would show that the costs of providing public education are greater because of larger staff sizes. This is precisely what they show. A study conducted at Virginia Polytechnic Institute and State University found that public colleges employ roughly 40 percent more labor than private colleges of the same size.[52] Differences in staff size were solely due to free-spending public-sector managers and cost-conscious private-sector supervisors.

Although the cost of providing public education has increased rapidly, there have been no improvements in student performance. Scholastic Aptitude Test scores have declined steadily while per pupil expenditures have skyrocketed. A recent Harvard University study found that, in high schools, the amount of educational spending per student had no effect on either educational attainment or occupational success.[53] Students from low-spending schools are just as likely to advance themselves as students from high-spending schools. The study also showed that large class sizes rather than small class sizes helped students toward both educational and occupational success. So the quality of education need not be reduced if school budgets were cut and class sizes increased.

The most effective way to improve educational performance is to rely more heavily on private-sector incentives. Competition brings about more cost-effective instruction methods. It also pressures institutions to offer high-quality programs. The facts show that a disproportionate number of the highest-quality colleges and universities in the United States are private.[54]

In spite of the success of private education, there has been a phenomenal expansion of public education at the expense of both private institutions and taxpaying Americans. Billions of federal, state, and local tax dollars have been poured into public education to subsidize tuition costs. Unfortunately, all that this spending seems to have done is to increase taxes and strangle private schools, which cannot compete with subsidized systems. Politicians, obviously, have supported the expansion of public education in America. However, political support has been based not on efficiency, but on egalitarian grounds. Increased spending on public education, it is argued, has promoted more equitable educational opportunities by making it possible for everyone to attend high school and college.

For years, economists have contended that to get equal educational opportunity, the government should issue vouchers to individuals that would allow them to attend the schools of their choice. Instead, government officials have sought to expand the size and scope of public education in order to solve the problem. In the words of Sen. Patrick Moynihan:

> In the contest between public and private education, the national government feigns neutrality, but it is in fact anything but neutral. As program has been piled atop program, and regulation on regulation, the federal government has systematically organized its activities in ways that contribute to the decay of nonpublic education. Most likely, those responsible have not recognized this; they think themselves blind to the distinction between public and private. But of course they are not. They could not be. For governments inherently, routinely, automatically favor creatures of government. They know no other way. They recognize the legitimacy of no other institution.[55]

The advantages of private over public enterprise are confirmed by all these studies of private-public production of refuse collection, fire protection, debt collection, ship repair, electric power generation, airline services, weather forecasting, ambulance services, and education. The Bureaucratic Rule of Two might not apply in every case, but there is clear evidence that huge savings could be achieved by turning many government activities over to private enterprise.

Labor Use and Productivity

The discussion of public- and private-sector managerial behavior in Chapter 3 suggests that bureaucrats use many more employees to do the same jobs as private enterprise. The preceding case study of education demonstrates the labor bias of the public sector. Recall that public colleges were found to employ 40 percent more labor than private colleges of equivalent size. A survey of Pennsylvania cities with populations between 24,000 and 400,000 showed that public trash collection required 97.3 percent more employees than private collection.[56] In addition, employment figures for public- and private-sector hospitals indicate that public facilities use much more labor than private hospitals, especially with respect to profit-seeking health-care facilities.

Critics of the labor-bias theory of government contend that public employment has not grown very rapidly, especially in the federal government, and that government actually employs large quantities of labor-saving equipment. The U.S. Civil Service Commission reported that the full-time civilian employment of the federal government was 2.48 million as of March 31, 1978, only a slight increase over the 2.24 million employees reported in 1959 (an annual percentage growth of only 0.69 percent).[57] Therefore, it is argued, government does not show a tendency to expand staff size. We do not accept that conclusion.

A closer look reveals that reported employment is only the tip of the bureaucratic iceberg. Government also employs a horde of consultants and contractors who often use government equipment and facilities and who simply represent an extension of the arm of government. For example, an article published in a Washington, D.C., public policy journal, *Policy Review*, contained the following statement:

A good estimate would be that from three to four million persons are paid by the federal government through consulting contracts, research grants, and payments made for the wages of state and local government employees. Secretary Joseph Califano of HEW recently testified to the Senate Appropriations Committee that his department pays the salaries of 980,217 persons who work for private think-tanks, universities, and state and local governments. This is in addition to the 144,256 "regular" HEW employees. The Department of Defense estimates that it pays the salaries of an additional 2,050,000 people through consulting contracts and the like. This figure does not include 2,049,000 military personnel who are also federal employees.[58]

A *National Journal* study estimated that 11 million persons were directly or indirectly employed by the federal government.[59] About one person in every eight in the labor force today is working directly or indirectly for the federal government.

There is, for the taxpayer, a big difference between full-time government employees and those who work indirectly for the government on contract. There is no long-term commitment by the government to any contract employee: termination (or cancellation) of the contract ends the government's obligation to the employee. Thus, salaries, fringe benefits, and pension costs are incurred only while the contract is in force. For this reason, private contractors provide all levels of government with a flexible work force which can easily be expanded or reduced to meet changing needs, even on a very short-term basis. With regular civil servants, this flexibility does not exist. Once a government employee has fulfilled the probationary period, the government (that is, the taxpayer), except in highly unusual circumstances, has to pay his salary and fringe benefits until he retires and his pension thereafter.

The employment statistics reported by the federal government do not include part-time employees or individuals on "special assignment" who are paid directly from the federal treasury. This allows the bureaucracy to avoid any employment ceilings on hiring. When employment ceilings are imposed on federal agencies, they restrict only the number of full-time employees. Each March 31 the agencies report their employment statistics. On the same date, thousands of people are switched from full-time to part-time status. These full-time–part-time bureaucrats are known throughout the federal government as "25-and-ones." For 25 of the 26 federal pay periods each year, the workers are classified as full time, but in the one pay period in which the headcount is taken, the workers are classified as part time. According to the *Washington Post*, "Nearly one out of every 20 workers in the civilian federal work force, excluding the Postal Service, holds a temporary, part-time or special assignment job that is not counted when the full-time government payroll is measured."[60] The part-time worker should not be confused with industry contract employees. In fact, Office of Management and Budget (OMB) circular A-76 specifically prohibits the use of contracting out to avoid employment ceilings.

Any statistics now available vastly understate the true number in the total federal work force. The most accurate statement that can be made about it is that its size is unknown.

In answer to those who assert that government uses larger quantities of capital, we must first distinguish between the acquisition of capital and its use. In the private sector, capital equipment is purchased to improve the productivity of labor in order to lower costs. In government, capital equipment is often purchased more to enhance the prestige of the office that acquires it than to increase efficiency. A case study illustrates this point. Between 1969 and 1977 the federal government spent more than $295.1 million on the rental and purchase of word-processing equipment.[61] If the same rate of expenditures is maintained, annual spending will exceed $300 million by 1982. Basically, these machines are memory typewriters that help make corrections and do editing. They are quite common in the private sector. This equipment should offer enormous potential for cost savings and manpower reductions. Having recognized this possibility, the General Accounting Office has stated:

> The federal government . . . employs over 171,000 secretaries, stenographers and typists. The annual salary outlay for these employees is over $1.5 billion. This secretarial force represents close to 11.5 percent of the total civilian white-collar work force. Even slight increases in secretarial

productivity would significantly lower the cost of this segment of the work force, thus making it particularly open to the application of word processing systems.[62]

The GAO undertook an audit of the use of this equipment in 10 agencies and various field offices to determine their cost effectiveness, because there was no evidence of a decline in secretarial or clerical staffing. Findings showed that most agencies could not demonstrate any increased productivity or cost effectiveness. The Internal Revenue Service had installed, over a five-year period, a number of machines that cost $71,000 in annual rental; some were used as little as 1.5 hours per day. The U.S. Office of Education, apparently as a result of the GAO audit, planned to return 60 word-processing systems because they were unnecessary.[63]

If, in fact, government uses capital equipment to increase efficiency and reduce costs, it is surprising that the evidence shows that the provision of goods and services by the public sector is far more costly than that by the private sector. There is no evidence that the productivity of government has increased as rapidly as that of the private sector.

Table 8

Estimates of Productivity in the
Federal Sector and in Manufacturing, by Year
1967–1970

	Unit labor costs (1967—base year)		Output per man-hour (1967—base year)	
	Federal Govt.	Manufacturing	Federal Govt.	Manufacturing
1967	100.0	100.0	100.0	100.0
1968	102.5	102.3	101.8	104.7
1969	108.5	106.6	103.4	106.9
1970	117.5	112.5	106.4	108.1

SOURCE: William Orzechowski, "Economic Models of Bureaucracy," *Budgets and Bureaucrats: The Sources of Government Growth*, ed. Thomas E. Borcherding (Durham, N.C.: Duke University Press, 1977), p. 251.

Studies at the Virginia Polytechnic Institute and State University show that productivity gains at all levels of government lag far behind those of the private sector, especially when it is realized that productivity measures for the government are probably overestimates.[64] Table 8 estimates productivity in the federal government from 1967 to 1970. Unit labor costs have risen in the federal sector more rapidly than in the private sector and increases in federal output per man-hour have lagged consistently behind those in the private sector.

More detailed estimates of the productivity of 28 federal government activities have been computed by the Department of Labor for the period 1967–77, as reported in Table 9. They show that productivity increased more slowly and unit labor costs more rapidly in the federal sector than the figures in Table 8 indicate. In only one of the 28 services did unit labor costs decline; in only five cases was the growth rate of output per employee greater than three percent per year. Overall, federal productivity increased at the modest rate of 1.3 percent per year while unit labor costs increased 7.2 percent annually.

As for state and local government, studies show that productivity increases have been even lower.[65] For the four local government services—police, fire, public welfare, and administration—the number of employees increased relative to services by 14.36, 11.13, 28.56, and 29.15 percent, respectively, during the period 1962–67. This is direct evidence that lagging productivity is a major factor in raising costs of state and local government. More recent statistics show that employment in state and local governments has increased rapidly.[66]

Conclusion

In most of our case studies no attempt was made to identify and account for the "opportunity costs" of public rather than private production. Thus, switching from the public to the private sector would bring government revenues which are not currently received. Private firms pay taxes and licensing fees at the federal, state, and local levels of government from which the public enterprise is exempt. Extremely burdensome government regulations inflict high costs on private firms, but public agencies are not required to comply. In addition, pension plans for government employees are rarely fully vested and represent

67

Table 9

Average Annual Rates of Change in Output Per
Employee-Year, Compensation Per Employee, and Unit
Labor Costs for 28 Federal Government Activities
Fiscal Years 1967–1977

Functional grouping	Average annual rate of change		
	Output per employee-year	Compensation per employee-year	Unit labor cost
Communications*	9.2	7.9	-1.1
Library service	5.4	8.2	2.7
Loans and grants	4.4	8.0	3.4
General support services	4.2	7.6	3.2
Personnel investigations	3.3	6.6	3.2
Social services and benefits	2.9	7.0	4.0
Records management	2.8	8.4	5.5
Transportation	2.6	8.7	6.0
Buildings and grounds maintenance	2.3	9.7	7.3
Regulation—rulemaking and licensing	2.3	6.7	4.3
Audit of operations	2.2	7.4	5.1
Regulation—compliance and enforcement	2.1	6.8	4.7
Supply and inventory control	2.1	7.6	5.4
Personnel management	2.0	5.2	3.1
Finance and accounting	1.8	7.5	5.6

Procurement	1.8	5.3	3.4
Specialized manufacturing	1.8	8.5	6.6
Electric power production and distribution	1.4	8.0	6.5
Natural resources and environmental management	1.2	7.2	5.9
Postal service	1.1	10.1	8.9
Legal and judicial activities	0.5	5.3	4.8
Equipment maintenance**	0.3	7.8	7.4
Information services	0.3	5.6	5.3
Traffic management†	0.3	5.6	5.2
Education and training**	0.2	8.2	8.0
Medical services	-0.1	8.0	8.1
Military base services	-0.6	7.5	8.2
Printing and duplication	-1.7	9.2	11.1
Total	1.3	8.7	7.2

SOURCE: U.S. Congress, Joint Economic Committee, *Productivity in the Federal Government* (Washington, D.C.: U.S. Government Printing Office, 1979), p. 6.

*Fiscal years 1973–77.
**Fiscal years 1968–77.
†Fiscal years 1972–77.

a substantial future tax liability. If these considerations had been taken into account in the cost comparison studies, private enterprise would have appeared even more efficient than government.[67]

NOTES TO CHAPTER 4

[1]Thomas E. Borcherding, "The Sources of Growth in Public Expenditures in the U.S. 1902–1970," *Budgets and Bureaucrats: The Sources of Government Growth,* ed. Thomas E. Borcherding (Durham, N.C.: Duke University Press, 1977), p. 62.

[2]Hearings Before the Small Business Administration, *Government Competition with Small Business,* Des Moines, Iowa, August 28, 1970.

[3]A complete discussion of the term *opportunity cost* is found in James D. Gwartney and Richard Stroup, *Economics: Private and Public Choice* (New York: Academic Press, 1980), pp. 22, 712–13.

[4]See John C. Perham, "The Mess in Public Pensions," *Dun's Review* (March 1976) p. 48.

[5]*Ibid.,* p. 49.

[6]*Ibid.*

[7]"Danger: Pension Perils Ahead," *Time* (September 24, 1979) pp. 68–69.

[8]U.S. Department of Commerce, Bureau of Economic Analysis, *Survey of Current Business* (July 1972).

[9]Harry H. Wellington and Ralph K. Winter, *The Unions and the Cities* (Washington, D.C.: Brookings Institution, 1971), pp. 19–20.

[10]Bernard Jump, "Compensating City Government Employees: Pension Benefits Objectives, Cost Measurement, and Financing," *National Tax Journal* (September 1976), p. 149.

[11]James T. Bennett and Manuel H. Johnson, *The Political Economy of Federal Government Growth* (College Station, Tex.: Center for Education and Research in Free Enterprise, Texas A & M University, 1980).

[12]*Ibid.*

[13]Werner Hirsch, "Cost Functions of Government Service: Refuse Collection," *Review of Economics and Statistics* (February 1973) pp. 85–93.

[14]Robert M. Spann, "Public Versus Private Provision of Governmental Services," *Budgets and Bureaucrats: The Sources of Government Growth,* ed. Thomas E. Borcherding (Durham, N.C.: Duke University Press, 1977), pp. 71–89.

[15]Peter Kemper and John M. Quigley, *The Economics of Refuse Collection* (Cambridge, Mass.: Ballinger Publishing Company, 1976).

[16]Barbara J. Stevens, "Scale, Market Structure, and the Cost of Refuse Collection," *Review of Economics and Statistics* (August 1978) pp. 438–48.

[17]Harry M. Kitchen, "A Statistical Estimation of an Operating Cost Function for Municipal Refuse Collection," *Public Finance Quarterly* (January 1976) pp. 56–57.

[18]For a more detailed discussion of budget accounting procedures, see James T. Bennett and Manuel H. Johnson, "Public Versus Private Provision of Collective Goods and Services: Garbage Collection Revisited," *Public Choice* (Spring 1979) pp. 55–63; Bennett and Johnson, "Tax Reduction Without Sacrifice: Private Sector Production of Public Services," *Public Finance Quarterly* (October 1980); and Ben-

nett and Johnson, "Paperwork and Bureaucratic Behavior," *Economic Inquiry* (July 1979) pp. 435–51.

[19]Kemper and Quigley, *op. cit.*, p. 57.

[20]*Ibid.*

[21]Bennett and Johnson, "Public Versus Private," pp. 55–63.

[22]Robert W. Poole, *Cut Local Taxes: Without Reducing Essential Services* (Santa Barbara, Calif.: Reason Press, 1976), pp. 18–19.

[23]"Improving Municipal Productivity," National Commission on Productivity and Work Quality (Washington, D.C.: National Commission on Productivity and Work Quality, 1976).

[24]Poole, *op cit.*, pp. 4–5.

[25]Mark Frazier, "Scottsdale Slashes Spending," *Reader's Digest* (February 1978).

[26]*Ibid.*

[27]Roger Ahlbrandt, "Efficiency in the Provision of Fire Services," *Public Choice* (Fall 1973) pp. 1–15.

[28]*Ibid.*, p. 11.

[29]*Ibid.*, p. 10.

[30]Poole, *op. cit.*, pp. 3–7.

[31]U.S. General Accounting Office, *The Government Can Be More Productive in Collecting Its Debts by Following Commercial Practices*, Report by Comptroller General of the United States: FGMSD-78-59 (February 23, 1979).

[32]*Ibid.*, p. i.

[33]*Ibid.*

[34]Ronald Kessler, "Duplicate Checks Cost U.S. Millions," *Washington Post* (November 6, 1979) p. A1.

[35]*Ibid.*

[36]U.S. General Accounting Office, *The Government Can Be More Productive*, p. iii.

[37]*Ibid.*

[38]U.S. General Accounting Office, *The Navy Overhaul Policy—A Costly Means of Insuring Readiness for Support Ships*, Report by Comptroller General of the United States: LCD-78-434 (December 27, 1978).

[39]*Ibid.*, pp. 27, 53–54.

[40]U.S. General Accounting Office, *Increased Productivity Can Lead to Lower Costs at Federal Hydroelectric Plants*, Report by Comptroller General of the United States: FGMSD-79-15 (May 29, 1979).

[41]*Ibid.*, p. i.

[42]*Ibid.*

[43]*Ibid.*, p. ii. The discussion of cost comparisons of public vs. private electric utilities is limited in the text to hydroelectric utilities. The private sector also has been found to be far more efficient than the public sector in electric generation at steam-powered facilities. An excellent survey of this literature may be found in Louis DeAlessi, "An Economic Analysis of Government Ownership Regulation: Theory and Evidence from the Electric Power Industry," *Public Choice* (Fall 1974) pp. 1–42. The concepts discussed in this paper might be somewhat difficult for a noneconomist, but the conclusion is unambiguous: the private sector outperforms the public sector by a wide margin in the production of electric power.

71

⁴⁴"Dividend from Deregulation," *Time* (December 12, 1979) p. 113.

⁴⁵The Australian airline case has been researched in considerable detail by David G. Davies, "Property Rights and Economic Efficiency—The Australian Airlines Revisited," *Journal of Law and Economics* (April 1977) pp. 223–26.

⁴⁶*Ibid.*, pp. 224–25, n. 10.

⁴⁷Paul Valentine, "Private Firm Hired to Replace National Weather Forecasters," *Washington Post* (July 19, 1979) p. A1.

⁴⁸Poole, *op. cit.*, pp. 6–7.

⁴⁹*Ibid.*, p. 7.

⁵⁰*Ibid.*, pp. 8–12.

⁵¹*Ibid.*, pp. 11–12.

⁵²William Orzechowski, "Economic Models of Bureaucracy," *Budgets and Bureaucrats: The Sources of Government Growth*, ed. Thomas E. Borcherding (Durham, N.C.: Duke University Press, 1977), pp. 257–59.

⁵³Christopher S. Jencks and Marsha D. Brown, "Effects of High Schools on Their Students," *Harvard Educational Review* (August 1975) pp. 270–83.

⁵⁴Waldemar A. Neilson, *The Endangered Sector* (New York: Columbia University Press, 1979), p. 96.

⁵⁵Daniel Patrick Moynihan, "Government and the Ruin of Private Higher Education," *Harper's* (April 1978) p. 26.

⁵⁶Poole, *op. cit.*, p. 19.

⁵⁷U.S. Civil Service Commission, *Federal Civilian Manpower Statistics: Pay Structure of the Federal Service* (Washington, D.C.: U.S. Government Printing Office, 1959, 1978).

⁵⁸Donald Lambro, "In and Out at HEW: Doing Well by Doing Good Through Consulting," *Policy Review* (Winter 1979) p. 109.

⁵⁹Barbara Blumenthal, "Uncle Sam's Army of Invisible Employees," *National Journal* (May 5, 1979) p. 732.

⁶⁰Kathy Sawyer, "Numbers Game in Bureaucracy: Thousands of Employees Hidden to Avoid Manpower Ceiling," *Washington Post* (August 16, 1979) p. A1.

⁶¹U.S. General Accounting Office, *Federal Productivity Suffers Because Word Processing Is Not Well Managed*, Report by Comptroller General of the United States: FGMSD-79-17 (April 6, 1979).

⁶²*Ibid.*, p. 34.

⁶³*Ibid.*

⁶⁴Orzechowski, *op. cit.*, p. 250.

⁶⁵See Robert M. Spann, "Rates of Productivity Change and the Growth of State and Local Government Expenditures," *Budgets and Bureaucrats: The Sources of Government Growth*, ed. Thomas E. Borcherding (Durham, N.C.: Duke University Press, 1977), pp. 100–129.

⁶⁶Roger A. Freeman, *The Growth of American Government: A Morphology of the Welfare State* (Stanford, Calif.: Hoover Institution Press, 1975), p. 208.

⁶⁷Although not discussed in detail in this book, there is considerable evidence that shows, without exception, that privately provided health-care services are less costly or are of higher quality than publicly provided health-care services. See Kenneth W. Clarkson, "Some Implications of Property Rights in Hospital Management," *Journal of Law and Economics* (October 1972) pp. 363–84; H.E. Frech, "The Property Rights Theory of the Firm: Empirical Results from a Natural Experiment," *Journal of Po-*

litical Economy (February 1976) pp. 143–52; see also Cotton M. Lindsay, ''A Theory of Government Enterprise,'' *Journal of Political Economy* (October 1976) pp. 1061–78.

5

THE CRITICS OF CONTRACTING OUT: IS GOVERNMENT FOR SALE?

The practice of contracting out public services to private firms has many critics. Public employees are the loudest because they have the most to lose. As pointed out in Chapter 3, bureaucrats have a vested interest in creating more government jobs. The more workers they can recruit to serve under them, the better their prospects for promotion and higher salaries.

Then there are the public employee unions. These unions generally do not organize and collect dues from workers in private firms. If they are to flourish, so must employment in the public sector. Contracting out is a clear threat to public employee unions such as the American Federation of State, County, and Municipal Employees (AFSCME) and the American Federation of Government Employees (AFGE). It is not surprising that in 1977 a book titled *Government for $ale: Contracting Out the New Patronage*, by John Hanrahan, was sponsored and published by AFSCME. This 307-page text reviews in great detail every known argument against contracting out.[1]

Hanrahan recognizes the conflict of interest that exists when a union of government employees finances such a study: "There is no question but that it is to AFSCME's advantage to keep contracting out to a minimum in order to protect jobs for AFSCME members" (p. 9); and "Of course, AFSCME has a vested interest in seeing that public service jobs are maintained for its members" (p. 245). Yet he would have his readers believe that turning to the private sector is even more costly:

The inescapable conclusion is that contracting out, far from being a potential financial boon for state and local governments, is a major source of government corruption, financial waste and inefficiency. In many cases it is a major cause of local governments' fiscal problems. In recent years some of the worst political scandals, some of the biggest fleecing of the taxpayers, were directly due to the contracting out of state and local government services—work which in most cases could have been performed more efficiently and at less cost by public employees. The overwhelming weight of the evidence shows that the more public officials deal with the business community, the more the taxpayer suffers—through graft, kickbacks, overcharges and poorer services.[p. 3]

This finding is in direct conflict with the studies in Chapter 4, which showed the private sector to be far more efficient than the public sector. The case studies we reported earlier were done by professional economists and government investigators who had no financial stake in their conclusions—unlike Hanrahan.

Regardless of whether or not one has an ax to grind in analyzing the economics of contracting out, let us look at the five basic criticisms Hanrahan makes:

1. *Corruption*—Corrupt politicians and greedy businessmen can rip off the taxpayer when contracting out is practiced.
2. *Efficiency*—The public sector, in fact, is more efficient than the private sector.
3. *Waste*—Much of the work performed by the private sector is useless.
4. *Compassion*—The public employee is motivated by compassion toward the needy, the sick, the elderly, and the poor; the private sector is motivated by greed.
5. *Economic Effects*—Contracting out creates unemployment and produces hardships for workers.

We'll take them one at a time.

76

Corruption: "It Takes Two to Tango"

No one would be shocked, or even mildly surprised, to be told that there are many corrupt politicians in this world. If public opinion polls have any validity, the public ranks the integrity of politicians on about the same level as that of used-car salesmen. Such attitudes are not new. More than half a century ago, H. L. Mencken acidly observed that politicians,

> in point of fact, are seldom, if ever, moved by anything rationally describable as public spirit; there is actually no more public spirit among them than among so many burglars or street-walkers. Their purpose, first, last, and all the time, is to promote their private advantage, and to that end, and that end alone, they exercise all the vast powers that are in their hands.[2]

Just as there are corrupt politicians, there are corrupt businessmen who overcharge for services, provide shoddy merchandise, and otherwise cheat the customer. According to the critics, contracting out brings the worst elements of both groups together by giving them unlimited opportunities for graft. The businessman submits an inflated contract to provide services for the public sector, which the politician makes sure is accepted. The politician is then rewarded with campaign contributions or outright kickbacks made possible by the "slush" funds in the contract. So both "get rich" while the taxpayers "get taken for a ride."

Such schemes unfortunately are common throughout the United States. Newspapers and news broadcasts all too frequently reveal instances where public funds are channeled through contracts for goods and services to corrupt businessmen who, in return, grease the palms of greedy politicians. In New York State the contracting out of trash collection, snow removal, street repair, landfill operations, vehicle maintenance, and other services has for years been riddled with kickbacks. Maryland became notorious through the antics of Spiro Agnew and his successor, Marvin Mandel, who was convicted of mail fraud during his term of office.

The federal government has also been rocked by scandals. In recent months, the procurement arm of the civil service, the General Services Administration, has been the center of investigation. It is interesting to note, however, that the individuals involved were not elected officials or even political appointees, but public employees.

Hundreds of millions of federal tax dollars were paid for goods that were never delivered. Government purchasing agencies routinely paid vastly inflated prices. Although the federal government buys items in large quantities and should have received substantial discounts, GSA approved many purchases at prices that were well above retail. Rents were paid on buildings that did not exist. In return, corrupt bureaucrats were given cash bribes, free vacations, and even the services of prostitutes. So widespread is corruption in the federal bureaucracy that a fraud ''hot line'' has been established in the General Accounting Office so that reports of corruption can be made toll-free and catalogued. Thus far, nearly 100 civil servants from GSA have been indicted and more investigations are in progress. It is obvious that public employees also have their hands in the public till. By no means can all the blame be placed on politicians and greedy businessmen. Further, although there may be smaller amounts of money and fewer people involved at state and local levels of government, many corrupt public employees are there as well.

How can such practices be avoided? The critics say the solution is simple: Political corruption can be eliminated if contracting out stops. But how can that work as long as public employees themselves are on the take? Political corruption is possible *only* if unscrupulous bureaucrats and politicians can connive with crooked businessmen. It has been shown repeatedly that sole-source contracting without competitive bidding is an open invitation to bilk the taxpayer. On a no-bid contract, it is simple for a corrupt politician and businessman to defraud the public by approving an inflated contract that provides a rake-off for the politician. The honest businessman is not even given an opportunity to bid.

Open, competitive bidding, in which the contract is awarded to the lowest bidder, is one solution. It is hardly surprising that the taxpayer is fleeced in contracting-out arrangements when the basic rules of sound business practice are flagrantly ignored. The *Washington Post* recently reported that ''sixty-eight percent of the 16,101 research and consulting contracts advertised [by the federal government in 1979] were awarded without competition.''[3] In the case of no-bid contracts, the undesirable results are caused not by a failure of the *private* sector at all, but by the *public* sector. Elected officials and public employees violate the public trust by not honestly managing public funds. To point an accusing finger at the private sector for the obvious failures of the officials and employees of the public sector is shabby and deceitful.

There is an even simpler way to avoid the political corruption that can accompany contracting out: eliminate the role of government altogether. Let the private sector meet community needs by contracting directly with individual citizens. Consider garbage collection. Hanrahan asserts in *Government for $ale*:

> Of all the municipal services that have been contracted out, none has been more beset with scandal, corruption, overcharge, rising rates and even Mafia infiltration than trash collection. In recent years there have been dozens of examples of price fixing, exorbitant charges, bribery, inefficiency, and financial waste connected with city garbage contracts—from Washington State to Florida, from New York to Illinois and Wisconsin. [p. 38]

Well then, if refuse collection is so open to abuse through political patronage, there is no reason why government needs to be involved in the collection process at all. Most communities already have health ordinances requiring homeowners and businesses to keep their premises free of trash. Let them contract with private firms to do the job, or haul their own trash to the dump if they so choose. This system is working well right now in the region where both authors live. In other parts of the area, where service is provided by public employees, the residents get only half as much service, but pay twice the price.[4]

Next let us consider the "voucher plan" for education originally proposed by Nobel laureate Milton Friedman in his book *Capitalism and Freedom*.[5] It is generally agreed that educating the nation's youth is socially desirable and that tax dollars should be used for this purpose. But there is no reason why government ought to be the provider of educational services. Friedman recommends that the schools themselves be private and that government should subsidize tuition and fees. Each household would be given a voucher worth a certain sum for each child of school age—the vouchers could be used only for educational purposes. Parents would then be free to choose from among competing private schools. If the parents became dissatisfied with the quality of instruction at one school, they could send their children elsewhere. Does anyone really believe that such a system could be worse than what presently exists?

The voucher system is not a pie-in-the-sky proposal, because it has worked successfully for years. The education benefits extended by the federal government to veterans are provided in voucher form, allowing the veteran to select the institution he wishes to attend and the course of study he wishes to pursue. Although as yet untried in practice, tax credits offer an even more appealing method of financing education: parents with children in school would be given a credit on their tax bills. The taxpayer is better off because a government bureaucracy is not required to collect taxes for educational purposes or to disburse vouchers. The inefficiency and waste of a government agency concerned with education can be avoided entirely. Only if public schools can get better results at lower costs than private schools can public schools be justified.

Bureaucratic Efficiency

The critics of contracting out rarely present hard evidence that bureaucrats can produce services at lower costs than the private sector. They consider it a foregone conclusion. After all, if contracting out is notoriously abused, one should not need to make cost comparisons to prove the point. If the money that goes for bribes, graft, and kickbacks is taken into account, public provision of essential services must logically be regarded as more efficient than the corrupt contract with the private sector. The *real* comparison, of course, is the one made where competitive bidding is allowed.

One of the most interesting examples of the "efficiency" of the public sector is cited by Hanrahan in *Government for $ales* to show that millions of dollars could be saved by having the trash at Chicago public schools collected by public employees.

In Chicago private collectors were apparently overcharging the Board of Education by one-half million dollars or more annually on $1.3 million worth of contracts to pick up the garbage at the city's public schools. Curiously enough, while the public schools were paying through the nose for garbage pickups, almost all of the city's private parochial schools were having their garbage picked up once a week free of charge by city crews! [p. 55]

The trash firms serving the public schools were charging more than twice the rate quoted to an investigator who requested quotations for similar collections from a hypothetical private school. Obviously, this is an excellent example of a political ripoff of the taxpayer that persisted over a long period of time: the arrangements between the city schools and the private firms had gone on for at least six years.

We do not question that the job could have been done for less. But what evidence is there to show that public employees could collect the school's trash at less cost than an honest private collector? The only support given is a finding from a report by a private watchdog organization which reads:

> It would take 15 additional trucks from the city's idle force of 300 to handle the school's garbage, freeing funds now spent on this service for teachers and programs. The City Sanitation Department is capable of accommodating public school garbage, just as it accommodates parochial school garbage.[6]

But wait a minute! If the public sector is so efficient, why does the city have no fewer than 300 trucks sitting idle? If the trucks were not needed, why were taxpayer funds spent to buy them in the first place? If they were once useful, but are no longer used, why doesn't the city get rid of them to save the costs of maintenance?

Surely not all the money paid to private refuse collectors can be saved for educational purposes for the simple reason that trash collection also requires manpower. Additional men have to be hired to haul trash—unless, of course, the city trash department also has a number of idle employees, just as it has idle trash trucks. If idle employees were available and could be used to collect school trash at no additional cost to the city, a natural question to ask is why were they on the payroll at all. An organization that pays workers for doing nothing can hardly be viewed as efficient.

Why, in half a dozen years, did no public employee in either the sanitation or the education department ever question the practice of contracting out? If the economies were so obvious, and if idle trucks and perhaps men were available, and if the private charges were so outlandish that significant savings could be realized, it seems bizarre that some budget analyst, supervisor, or other bureaucrat did not detect and expose this year-in, year-out fleecing of the taxpayer.

Perhaps these public servants were too busy looking out for themselves. Bureaucratic conceptions of efficiency are apt to be self-serving, as the following example indicates:

> Inglewood, California, has used one-man refuse trucks for more than a decade at significantly reduced cost and with fewer injuries and greater satisfaction for personnel. Informed of the one-man trucks, the sanitation director in an eastern city using four men to a truck said he did not believe it. Having confirmed that they were in use, he opined that Inglewood's streets and contours were different from his city's. Convinced that conditions in both places were generally the same, he lamented that his constituents would never accept the lower level of service. Persuaded that the levels of service were equal, he explained that the sanitation men would not accept a faster pace and harder work conditions. Told that the Inglewood sanitation men prefer the system because they set their own pace and suffer fewer injuries caused by careless coworkers, the director prophesied that the city council would never agree to such a large cutback in manpower. Informed of Inglewood's career development plan to move sanitation men into other city departments, the director pointed out he was responsible only for sanitation.[7]

Federal employees are even more cavalier in their handling of the taxpayers' money. According to the *Washington Post* (December 20,

1979), "The federal government stores enough furniture to fill the Pentagon and take care of government needs for 10 years while it continues to buy $200 million in new furniture a year. . . . " In the Washington, D.C., area alone, furniture is stored at 76 different locations (one of which is a nine-story warehouse) and it costs the taxpayers a fortune each year to rent and maintain the 3.7 million square feet of storage space. Millions of dollars' worth of furniture has disappeared.

If this is bureaucratic efficiency, it is impossible to believe that the private sector could do much worse. If, as the critics of contracting out contend, the major concern of the public employee is the public interest, why are there so many cases in which public employees failed to act in behalf of the taxpayers or were directly responsible for the misuse of funds? The answer, as we have suggested before, is that bureaucrats have no incentive to be efficient or economical when they are rewarded for waste.

Contract Waste: Boon and Boondoggles

Probably no one will ever be able to count the number of worthless projects government has paid the private sector to undertake, or accurately estimate their cost. There are simply too many nooks and crannies of virtually every agency, bureau, commission, and department of government to investigate. Yet, many are exposed. Whether the exposure stems from Sen. William Proxmire's Golden Fleece Award, or the efforts of a tenacious reporter, or through some other means, it is not unusual to pick up a newspaper and find still another boondoggle revealed.[8] One day the newspaper might feature a National Science Foundation grant to study the rectal temperature of hibernating bears. The next, it might publicize a National Endowment for the Arts award to an "artist" for the purpose of creating "dynamic art" by throwing colored streamers out of an airplane. And on the third day, an article might appear about a research contract to investigate the reasons children fall off tricycles. (The researcher's conclusion—"They lose their balance.")

Critics of contracting out cite numerous examples of worthless projects as evidence that private contracts cause waste of public funds.[9]

They argue that private firms are awarded the contracts, private firms spend the contract money, and private firms produce the valueless results. If there were no contracts, the argument continues, there would be no contract waste. Therefore, contracting should be abolished or at least severely restricted.

Tortured logic? Certainly. In fact, we will paraphrase the preceding paragraph using different subject matter to show just how absurd the argument is:

> Critics of automobiles cite numerous examples of traffic accidents as evidence that automobiles cause personal injury. They argue that automobiles are heavy objects, automobiles travel at high speeds, and automobiles injure people. If there were no automobiles, the argument continues, there would be no traffic accidents. Therefore, automobiles should be abolished or at least severely restricted.

Virtually anything—automobiles, fire, knives, morphine, and contracts—can be good or bad. It is the way things are used that determines whether something is a boon or a boondoggle. Obviously, if there were no automobiles, there would be no traffic accidents. But then neither would there be all the benefits we have experienced because of automobiles, The same is true of contracts. If there were no contracts, there would be no boondoggles. But then neither would there be the important cost savings derived from the contracting process. As with everything else, it is essential to separate the useful contract from the wasteful one to ensure that the taxpayer receives fair value for tax dollars: *this is the job of the public employee.*

Clearly, the private sector could not waste money on useless contracts if the contracts were not given by bureaucrats in the first place. It is not the private firm that solicits contract proposals; it is the bureaucrat. It is not the private firm that reviews contract proposals; it is the bureaucrat. It is not the private firm that awards the contract; it is the bureaucrat. It is not the private firm that monitors the work performed once a contract is awarded; it is the bureaucrat. The message cannot be overemphasized: *the source of contract waste is the public sector, not the private sector.*

Boondoggles occur only because bureaucrats cannot effectively manage the funds under their control and because they have money to waste. As pointed out in Chapter 3, a spending spree occurs at the end of each fiscal year as each agency gets rid of all the funds appropriated for its operations so it can ask for more the next fiscal year. The important objective is to spend the agency's surplus—on good contracts or bad. It is not surprising in a crash spending program that marginal, submarginal, and worthless contracts are approved. Rather than accept the responsibility for their own failures, the bureaucrats find it far more convenient to place the blame on the private sector for the resulting boondoggles.

Congress has long known about the bureaucrats' annual orgy of spending. Finally, after scandals occurred in a series of contracts to consulting firms located around Washington, it decided to act. So what have our lawmakers tried to do? Reduce the budget of offending agencies? No. Penalize or reward government managers on performance? No. Require an agency at least to have the decency to waste money more evenly throughout the year rather than in a last-minute splurge? Yes, to some extent. Reduce the use of contracts? Of course.

One of the most extreme examples of contract waste cited by the critics of contracting out involves the enormous cost overruns associated with the DD-963 Destroyer program.[10] The U.S. Navy contracted with the Ingalls Shipbuilding Division of Litton Industries in Pascagoula, Mississippi, for the construction of 30 destroyers. The overruns exceeded $800 million on a $1.8 billion contract. On the surface, these simple facts seem to provide a devastating indictment of contracting out. Before drawing any conclusions, however, let's delve deeper into the matter and look at the role of the bureaucracy.

Some time before the DD-963 program, the navy ended the construction of all *new* ships at U.S. naval shipyards for the simple reason that the costs in private yards were much, much lower. Today, naval shipyards are engaged only in overhaul and repair because they are not competitive with the private sector. In addition, much of the overhaul and repair work is contracted out because the naval yards are not efficient.

Contracts with private firms do not materialize out of thin air. In the case of naval contracts, invitations to bid are issued and firms respond with bid proposals. Each bid proposal is, in theory, carefully evaluated by a "pre-award audit," in which a group of government employees visits the site and makes an assessment of the bidder's ability to perform the work in accordance with the costs and time schedules set fourth in the bid proposal. If the pre-award audit indicates that either the cost figures or the time schedules are unrealistic, then adjustments must be made or the bidder is disqualified from receiving the contract.

In the Litton case, once the contract was awarded, the contractor's performance was monitored continually. Periodic production audits were scheduled (in which one of the authors of this book participated as a consultant) and an experienced team of public employees of the navy was sent from Washington to the shipbuilding facility to assess the progress. On a day-to-day basis, dozens of government employees were stationed at the Litton facility to audit the contract. Government auditors were also stationed at the facility. The first floor of the Litton administration building was occupied by company personnel, but the entire second floor was taken by offices of government personnel whose only job was to ensure contract compliance on a daily basis.

Under such conditions, how could these huge overruns occur, given such careful attention to the execution of the contract? Naval personnel at the shipyard were all well aware of the performance of Litton on the destroyer contract—indeed, they were literally "sitting on top" of the shipbuilder. Millions of dollars were spent by the government in supervising the contractor's performance; if fraud was practiced, why was it not uncovered? If fraud was uncovered, why weren't the claims disallowed and not paid? The answer is simple: the government was directly responsible for many of the problems contributing to the overruns. The navy encourages contractors to underbid or understate the true costs of weapons systems, including ships, so that it is easier to obtain political support for the funds necessary to buy them. If congressmen were aware of the true cost at the outset, they might balk at providing the funding. Once a contract is awarded, it is not uncommon for thousands of changes to be requested in design or even in the delivery schedule. These alterations further increase the cost.

Government Compassion: Bureaucrats Have Hearts

The critics of public contracting to the private sector are particularly vocal when services for the poor, sick, elderly, and disabled are involved. The argument seems to be that compassion and profits are incompatible; the private sector, motivated solely by "greed," cannot possibly provide the type of services required. Only bureaucrats, they allege, truly "care" about the needs of the disadvantaged.

In *Government for $ale,* Hanrahan focuses on nursing homes:

> The nation's private nursing home industry, as has been well-documented in many studies, investigations and books, is a disgrace. As Mary Adelaide Mendelson's book, *Tender Loving Greed,* described it, the nursing home business "mistreats the old and helpless and, swallowing tax money, robs us all" while the government "through the very munificence of [its] aid, together with the lack of effective government control, has made the nursing home industry into a giant profit machine which has attracted not only thousands of small-time hustlers but the big-money manipulators as well." [p. 155]

Admittedly, there are some corrupt nursing home operators, just as there are corrupt politicians, bureaucrats, and businessmen. To protect the public from dishonest operators, most states adopt standards for their operation. Such standards are given the force of law, in that operators who fail to comply can be fined and forced out of business. If nursing homes do not meet minimal state standards, it must be because they were not enforced. Who is supposed to enforce them? That's the job of the public sector. If deplorable conditions are widespread in the nursing home industry when state standards are present, the failure lies with the bureaucrats. They, and the politicians, are not very "compassionate" where the interests of the elderly are concerned.

The record of protecting the poor from ripoffs is miserable. In 1975 an organization in Washington, D.C., Pride Incorporated, acquired an apartment complex from the Department of Housing and Urban Development (HUD). In stories reported by the *Washington Post* (October 22–24, 1979) it was revealed that financial irregularities were commonplace. Over a four-year period, Pride, Inc., made only four mortgage payments and, according to the *Post,* "three top P.I. officials systematically diverted or stole at least $600,000." Pride failed to make needed repairs on the apartments and did not, at the time, provide

heat and other essential services for the tenants, who complained frequently.

HUD was well aware of the problems, but waited *two and one-half years* before so much as sending auditors to check the firm's records. Even though officials of Pride were under indictment for fraud, the Department of Labor awarded a $1.34 million contract to the firm!

Although the actions of Pride certainly must be condemned, so must the failure of public officials to correct such abuses promptly. No private lender would have dallied for years over the default on mortgage payments. The reason that the abuses were so severe is that the federal bureaucracy failed to do its job.

In fact, bureaucratic bungling is the root cause of many of the problems that exist in dealing with the poor. In Illinois and some other states, doctors use collection agencies to obtain payment of medicaid bills.[11] Physicians sometimes increased their bills to cover the cost of collection agency fees. Thus, it appears that bills for medical treatment under medicaid programs are inflated, and that this program to aid the poor is being ripped off by private physicians.

But why do collection agencies get involved in health care at all? The reason is that bureaucrats were not paying the physicians' bills. Doctors had to wait for months to receive payment from the government. Public employers were inexcusably slow in paying them. Collection agencies that, in some cases, also were found to be inflating medicare bills, were able to develop a "rapport" with the bureaucratic agencies and could get prompt payment. The conclusion, therefore, is that bureaucrats found it more profitable to deal with collection agents than with individual doctors. Had public employees efficiently processed claims, doctors would not have had to resort to collection agencies, would not have adjusted their bills to cover collection fees, and the agencies would not have had any opportunity to alter medical bills. The problem was created by the public sector, not the private sector. If blame is to be placed anywhere for this "feeding off the poor," it must be directed squarely at rapacious or inefficient public employees.

Those who are feeding off the poor, the elderly, the sick, and the disadvantaged are tens of thousands of bureaucrats at the federal, state, and local levels of government. These highly paid and underworked public employees have created a health and welfare industry to manipulate. Tens of billions of tax dollars have been, and still are, spent on hundreds of programs with little effect. The number of welfare recipients has not declined and, if the critics of contracting out are correct, little progress has been made in improving conditions for health and nursing care. Clearly, the bureaucrat has been all too willing to ignore the failures in the public sector and content with pointing the finger of blame at the private sector. Such machinations serve the purpose of the bureaucrat by enhancing the size and scope of government.

Whither the Whistleblowers

Just for the fun of it, let us assume that public employees are efficient, honest, and truly concerned with the public interest and the welfare of the taxpayers. If they are all these things, it seems unlikely that corruption, graft, kickbacks, and waste (which the critics of contracting out claim are so prevalent) could persist for so long. Would it be possible for Litton Industries allegedly to waste nearly $800 million before anyone noticed? Could political corruption be so widespread in Albany, New York, for decades, without a public employee at some time or other catching on? Did it really escape the attention of Housing and Urban Development employees for more than three years that mortgage payments were not being made? Could dozens of employees at the General Services Administration be filling their pockets from the public purse for years without their coworkers' knowledge?

It is revealing that reports of corruption are rarely initiated by public employees themselves. They originate from citizen action groups, reporters, special prosecutors, or grand juries. Bureaucrats rarely blow the whistle on wrongdoing in government. To believe that political corruption is limited to elected politicians and political appointees is naive. The record shows that career civil servants at all levels of government are highly adept at bilking the taxpayer. When the bureaucrat has a choice of serving his own self-interest or of serving the interests of the taxpayers, there is little doubt as to which he'll do.

Neither can politicians be counted on to police activities in the public sector. If a politician "probes in the mud," there is always a risk he'll be spattered. It is in the interest of the party in power to cover up and minimize exposure of waste and corruption. Even the politicians in the minority party recognize the political power of government employees. Those in the public sector serve their private self-interest first and foremost. They are "all heart." That's why taxpayers suffer.

Economic Consequences of Contracting Out

When work previously done by government is contracted to private firms, jobs are reduced in the public sector and are created in the private sector. The critics of contracting out would have the public believe that public-sector workers are displaced and put on the unemployment rolls. Contracting out, however, does not cause jobs to disappear; on the contrary, jobs are created. Consider this hypothetical case. Suppose that work requiring 100 public employees is shifted from the public sector and that the more efficient private sector needs only 60 workers to do the job. A total of 100 public-sector workers are displaced, but if they are efficient, conscientious, and hardworking, these workers will have no difficulty in obtaining alternative employment. Many of them could, by choice or by contract arrangement, be hired by the private contractor. In fact, OMB Circular A-76, the federal government's policy statement on contracting out, states explicitly that "the contractor will give federal employees, displaced as a result of conversion to contract performance, the right of first refusal for employment openings on the contract for positions for which they are qualified." The taxes saved by having only 60 private rather than 100 public workers doing the work could be returned to the taxpayers, who would spend the money for goods and services they want, and thereby create the need for additional workers in the private sector. More goods and services would be produced and consumed, so that more income would be produced. Taxes would be lower, so that the taxpayer could decide how to spend more of his income rather than have the decisions made by a bureaucrat.

Government waste and inefficiency, it is true, do create jobs—more employees are required to accomplish a task than would be required in the private sector. These extra jobs, however, are in reality a welfare program in which waste and laziness are rewarded. The cost to the taxpayer of such shenanigans is far more than the tax dollars required

92

to pay bureaucratic salaries. Bureaucrats, to justify their existence, impose regulations, paperwork, and other burdens on private firms and individuals. The problem is not just that many government employees do little good, but that they do much harm.

Another criticism of contracting out is that the private sector "keeps wages low." Low bids are accomplished by "underpaying workers." But firms in the private sector cannot "keep wages low." Slavery was abolished in the United States more than a century ago: no worker can be forced to work on any job. If a worker can obtain better pay in another job, he is free to quit and take it. Private firms must pay going wage rates to attract and retain employees. It is true that wages and salaries in the private sector are considerably below the wages and salaries in the public sector. An extensive investigation of the salary structure in the federal government has shown that individuals with comparable skills were paid as much as 20 percent more in federal government than in the private sector in 1975.[12] This means that government employees are *grossly overpaid,* not that private-sector workers are *underpaid.* In reality, one of the important reasons why much of the work now done by government should be contracted out to private firms is that bureaucrats have managed, through their political activities, to raise their wage rates well above the competitive labor markets. The impoverished taxpayer must pay the bill.

When jobs are switched from the private to the public sector, however, the argument against "keeping wages low" seems to vanish. In *Government for $ale,* Hanrahan relates a tale about streetlights in Boston.[13] Boston Edison, a private utility, had a contract with the city to install and maintain streetlights. By law, the utility was required to use licensed electricians to do the work. The law did not apply to municipal governments, so that the city was able to use inexperienced workers to install streetlights and pay them less. Hanrahan makes no mention of the unemployed electricians in the private sector, nor does he complain about the low wages paid. He merely says that the public sector was a lower-cost producer. It escaped Hanrahan's attention, of course, that Boston Edison could also have used lower-paid inexperienced workers had the city not prohibited the company from doing so

NOTES TO CHAPTER 5

[1]John D. Hanrahan, *Government for $ale: Contracting Out the New Patronage* (Washington, D.C.: American Federation of State, County, and Municipal Employees, 1977).

[2]H. L. Mencken, *Prejudices* (New York: Random House, 1919), p. 180.

[3]Jonathan Neumann and Ted Gup, "Epidemic of Waste in U.S. Consulting Research," *Washington Post* (June 22, 1980) p. 1.

[4]See James T. Bennett and Manuel H. Johnson, "Public Versus Private Provision of Collective Goods and Services: Garbage Collection Revisited," *Public Choice* (Spring 1977) pp. 55–63.

[5]Milton Friedman, *Capitalism and Freedom* (Chicago: University of Chicago Press, 1962), pp. 85–107. See also Milton Friedman and Rose Friedman, *Free to Choose* (New York: Harcourt Brace Jovanovich, 1980), pp. 158–75.

[6]Hanrahan, *op. cit.*, p. 56.

[7](R. Scott Fosler) *Improving Productivity in State and Local Government: A Statement by the Research and Policy Committee for Economic Development* (New York, March 1976), p. 46.

[8]See William Proxmire, *The Fleecing of America* (New York: Houghton Mifflin, 1980).

[9]Bureaucrats are professionals when it comes to large-scale waste of tax money. For an eye-opening study of government waste, an excellent book is Donald Lambro's *Fat City: How Washington Wastes Your Taxes* (Chicago: Regnery/Gateway, 1980).

[10]Hanrahan, *op. cit.*, pp. 225–27.

[11]*Ibid.*, pp. 149–89.

[12]Sharon P. Smith, *Equal Pay in the Public Sector: Fact or Fantasy* (Princeton, N.J.: Princeton University Press, 1977), p. 132.

[13]Hanrahan, *op. cit.*, pp. 246 ff.

6

GOVERNMENT PROCUREMENT: POLICY VERSUS PRACTICE

The superior efficiency of the private sector has not gone unnoticed by some policymakers of the federal government. In March 1966 the Bureau of the Budget (now the Office of Management and Budget) issued Circular A-76, which announced a policy of relying upon private enterprise to provide for the needs of the executive branch, except where it is in the national interest to have the government do it. At state and local levels there are very few resolutions similar to Circular A-76 and they vary widely from state to state and community to community. California, North Carolina, Arkansas, Utah, Montana, Arizona, Mississippi, Tennessee, and Texas are bound by law or legislative resolution to rely on the private sector for goods and services.

Unfortunately, the adoption of a policy by elected representatives and its implementation by career bureaucrats are two entirely different matters. It is safe to say that bureaucrats are hostile toward more efficient private firms simply because these firms pose a threat to the jobs of government employees doing similar work. Many government agencies, therefore, engage in subversive activities against private competitors by hobbling them with regulations, inaccurately reporting costs, lobbying against them, and otherwise sabotaging their operations.

The bureaucracy has also usurped traditional private-sector functions. As a result, federal government expenditures have grown at an average annual rate of 14.5 percent between 1969 and 1978, while federal procurement spending has grown by only 6 percent annually over the same period.[1] A special report to the U.S. Office of Management and Budget in 1971 revealed that 18,618 government activities

95

duplicated a product or service available from private industry. These in-house activities required a capital investment of $10 billion and an annual operating cost of $10 billion.[2] These figures would be far higher if they took into account other areas not covered in the reports—activities (1) providing a product or service for the general public, (2) excluded by agency regulations, and (3) omitted by agency interpretation. These, to name but a few, are photographic services, printing and reproduction, communications, clothing manufacture, aircraft and automotive repair, road construction and maintenance, instrumentation, and fabrication.

Government enterprise is intruding into the engineering, design, and development of new products and systems, prototype fabrication, production, and overhaul and repair of hardware produced by industry. Obviously, every dollar of services produced by government represents an opportunity lost to private, taxpaying firms—especially to new, small firms. How can a new private firm compete with a public enterprise subsidized heavily by taxes, exempt from much of the burdensome paperwork and regulation, and which pays no taxes, purchases no licenses, and pays no government fees?

Government Procurement Policy

Circular A-76 indicated a firm commitment by the executive branch to rely on private enterprise to supply its needs. In addition, it stated that "no executive agency will initiate a 'new start' to continue the operation of an existing 'government commercial or industrial activity' except as specifically required by law or as provided in this circular." There were originally five circumstances under which the government might provide a commercial or industrial product or service for its own use: (1) when not to do so will disrupt or materially delay an agency's program; (2) when it has to be done for combat support or for training of military personnel or to strengthen mobilization readiness; (3) when a satisfactory commercial source is not available in time to get the job done; (4) when the product or service is available from another federal agency; and, (5) when using private firms will result in higher costs. In determining the costs of providing goods and services in-house, an agency was required to consider the cost of (1) personnel services and benefits; (2) materials, supplies, and utility services; (3) maintenance and repair; (4) damage or loss of property; (5) federal taxes forgone; (6) interest charges; and, (7) indirect costs.

A revision of Circular A-76 in August 1976 simplified the earlier version into three criteria: lack of satisfactory source, military necessity, and relative cost. The revision also established basic principles to be followed and detailed guidance in a *Cost Comparison Handbook.* These included use of firm bids or proposals to establish commercial costs, regulation of overhead and indirect costs for government operations, standard cost factors for government employee fringe benefits and administration of contracts, and additional costs that must be incurred before giving government work to private firms.

Under the old rules of A-76, federal agencies sharply underestimated the cost of providing retirement benefits for government workers engaged in in-house work. A department or agency computed its wage bill and then added 7 percent for employee retirement costs. This 7 percent was so out of date that the U.S. Civil Service Commission determined, in 1976, that it should be 24.7 percent—over three times the previously used percentage. If this revised policy was effectively administered, the saving to American taxpayers would be tremendous. According to Rep. Jack Kemp, the new rules would affect about 10,000 commercial and industrial operations currently provided by the federal government. The Department of Commerce has estimated that services representing approximately $3 billion could be switched to the private sector. Following the Bureaucratic Rule of Two, taxpayer savings should amount to $1.5 billion annually, no insignificant sum.[3]

Opposition to this new rule quickly surfaced. Government bureaucrats and public employee unions strongly resisted the revised circular, since a number of public-sector jobs would be eliminated. However, federal employees have no right to their jobs if there is no need for them. They are protected against political discrimination through the career civil service system, but their jobs are no more guaranteed—nor should they be—than jobs in the private sector. That is why there is an orderly process within the civil service for reductions in force. If the people adopt the attitude that everyone now holding a federal job is entitled to keep it, this country will never be able to reduce the size of government and its cost to the taxpayer.

At this writing, there is no counterpart to Circular A-76 for agencies under the supervision of the U.S. Congress, although the General

Accounting Office has recommended that Congress mandate a preference for the private sector.[4]

Much of the increase in government competition with private business has also resulted in growth in state and local government, indirectly fueled by the federal government. A great many federal dollars are spent supporting state and local activities. A current estimate places the number of state and local employees whose livelihood depends on federal dollars at five million.[5] Federal aid to the states from 1974 to 1978 was $301 billion, not including federal administrative expenses, grants directly to profit-making institutions, individuals and certain nonprofit institutions, payments for basic research, payments to cover administrative expenses for regional bodies, and other funds not redistributed to the states.[6]

This kind of aid has increased steadily over the years because of intensified lobbying by state and local officials for increased revenue-sharing funds. It also arises from greater competition for various block grants and grants-in-aid. The point is that funds granted to the state and localities frequently are used to support government commercial and industrial activities. The result is more competition with local taxpaying businesses. States and municipalities are not subject to revised Circular A-76, or any other related federal policies.

Government Procurement in Practice

The entrenched government bureaucracy is fighting private-sector production of public services on another front—through the political process. A recent bill introduced by Rep. Herbert Harris, a Democrat from Virginia, would have the effect of shifting more work to government employees rather than encouraging contracting out. Harris is politically beholden to federal government bureaucrats and government employee unions: he serves a congressional district in the Virginia suburbs of Washington, D.C., where the population is overwhelmingly composed of federal employees. Other proposed legislation includes the Department of Defense authorization bill that completely excludes research and development services used by DOD from the scope of Circular A-76. Also, the Labor-HEW Appropriations Act for fiscal year 1980 places a dollar ceiling on HEW's acquisition of outside consulting services.

In addition, federal agencies have tried to undermine Circular A-76 by unfairly competing with private businesses that offer the same goods or services. The following cases of both direct and indirect competition were taken from hearings held by the U.S. Small Business Administration in Des Moines, Iowa, on August 28, 1979.

Military Post Exchanges. The military exchange system does about $9 billion worth of business each year and receives about $130 million of federal subsidy annually. Exchanges were originally created to provide unobtainable items for military personnel in isolated areas who received very low wages. Today there is virtually no consumer product that cannot be found at some military post exchange—isolated or not. Moreover, exemptions under U.S. antitrust law make it possible for military exchanges to buy merchandise directly from manufacturers at lower costs than private firms dealing in the same quantities can. Further, exchanges are free from collecting sales taxes and are subsidized in order to offer deferred payment plans to customers at no interest.

The military exchange serving the Quantico Marine base in Quantico, Virginia, consistently violated government regulations prohibiting the sale of business suits. This activity was damaging to small clothing retailers in that area because it deprived local businesses of revenue that Congress intended they receive. When issued a restraining order, the Marine Corps acknowledged that it was violating regulations and said it would stop selling business suits when its supplies ran out. Imagine a small business in the private sector of the economy that was engaged in deceptive trade practices telling the Federal Trade Commission such practices would be stopped when supplies ran out.

According to testimony, "The problem is that you have a nine-billion-dollar industry administered by the military, regulated by the military, and investigated by the military, and completely insensitive to the needs of the local merchant." In Quantico, Virginia, alone, approximately 20 firms have been driven out of business by unfair post exchange competition in the last 15 years.

Over the course of a year, the Quantico exchange netted $250,000 from the sale of business suits. The loss of this business to local menswear retailers has meant the difference between success and failure. To top that off, the commanding general of the base at Quantico directed monies from the sale of suits at the post exchange into the recreational fund. Thus, funds that should rightfully have gone to local retailers were used to support such Quantico military priorities as a lush 18-hole golf course, swimming clubs, stables, and officer and NCO clubs.

Even though it has no current authority to sell business suits, the exchange system is now attempting to acquire that authority under-handedly. The U.S. Small Business Administration testimony showed that in March 1975 the exchange system was given authority, for the first time, to sell leisure-suit-type articles. However, the House Armed Services Committee specifically warned that this did not include the right to sell business suits. Despite this, the exchange system devised a scheme to sell business suits. In August 1979 the military exchange submitted a proposed revision of the definition of men's multipiece suits for approval by the House Armed Services Committee. The revised definition would permit the military to sell any type of men's suit it desired as long as a second contrasting pair of trousers were included.

In addition to the illegal sale of business suits, testimony from SBA hearings indicate that the Quantico military exchange also extended no-interest credit to patrons well beyond the limits imposed by Congress. In 1979 the House Armed Services Committee permitted the military exchange system to offer credit to buy uniforms and their accessories. The maximum credit could not exceed $250 over a six-month period. However, in November 1980 the Quantico exchange set up an unprecedented deferred payment program for the purchase of uniforms and accessories, which allowed up to $1,800 of credit, at no interest, over a 12-month period. This directive devastated local merchants who dealt in uniform sales. The Quantico exchange had over a half-million dollars' worth of deferred payment uniform sales on its books a short time after the base directive was issued. When the commanding general at Quantico was informed that he was violating a congressional directive, he stated that he had no intention of stopping this policy. It took a congressional investigation by Rep. Dan Daniel, chairman of the Non-Appropriated Fund Panel of the House Armed Services Committee, to force the commanding general to back down. Although this unauthorized credit plan was stopped, a significant amount of harm was done to local merchants. Most small businesses in the United States cannot afford to extend credit on large amounts of money at no interest over long periods of time. Only the huge subsidies given to the exchange system by the military, which come out of the taxpayer's pocket, make it possible for post exchanges to compete unfairly with private businesses.

Government Printing Facilities. Federal government printing policy is determined by the U.S. Congress. All federal printing and binding work must be performed by the Government Printing Office (GPO) unless the Joint Committee on Printing decides otherwise. In addition to the GPO, there are approximately 292 federal printing plants. They are exempt from cost comparisons required in Circular A-76.

In 1978 the federal printing budget was $1.1 billion, of which about one half was for GPO operations. The remaining $600 million went to other government agencies for their own printing needs. These agencies could either print their material in-house or contract it out to the private sector.

Much of the work performed by the GPO is for Congress and requires overnight printing for published daily records. Manpower demands of this nature cannot profitably be met by private firms if the costs are held to a reasonable level. Therefore, massive amounts of daily printing can only be done by the GPO and are not subject to competition from commercial firms. However, large amounts of other printing work performed by GPO and various federal agencies can be provided much more cheaply by the private sector. The Small Business Administration has concluded that small private businesses could provide much of the federal government's printing requirements at far lower costs and that most government printing operations should be subject to Circular A-76.[7]

Unfortunately, because in-house government printing is exempt from the requirements of A-76, printing facilities proliferate in the federal bureaucracy at the expense of the American taxpayers. There is no incentive whatever for efficiency because they have no competition.

Virtually all commercial establishments operate on multiple shifts to use fully the printing machinery and reduce unit costs. Most government facilities operate on only one shift. When the additional overhead, power, and related expenses are included, the cost of in-house government printing far exceeds that of the private sector. The taxpayer loses money twice when the government prints; first through the inaccurate computation of costs, and second through lost tax revenues that would be collected from commercial firms.

U.S. Postal Service. Recently the U.S. Postal Service proposed an amendment to the Private Express Statutes that would bring unaddressed circulars under its jurisdiction. Such an extension of its monopoly power would destroy a large number of private marketing-distribution firms. According to witnesses appearing at Small Business Administration hearings, there is a huge demand by magazine publishers for the services of private delivery firms. Magazine publishers contract with private delivery services to distribute their magazines at prices they can afford.

For example, *Better Homes and Gardens* utilizes a special marketing approach by which carriers that distribute the magazines are authorized to deliver unaddressed advertising material to subscribers. This arrangement reduces distribution costs to *Better Homes and Gardens* with each advertising piece delivered. The magazine charges distributors two cents per household if they include unaddressed advertising with delivery of the magazine. The local distributor charges *Better Homes and Gardens* 12 cents per magazine delivered, so that the net delivery cost to the magazine publisher is 10 cents per copy, a saving of 17 percent. The price charged the advertiser by the delivery service is about 8.6 cents per circular per household. For the advertiser to reach those same households with the same circular through the U.S. mail would cost a minimum of 14 cents per household—six cents for the sorting and selecting services and eight cents for third-class postage.

This marketing-distribution arrangement increases the gross revenue per magazine delivered from 12 cents to 20.5 cents and allows a net profit of 8.5 cents. Thus, each local advertising piece adds 6.5 cents to the net revenue of the delivery service while diminishing the net delivery cost to *Better Homes and Gardens* by 2 cents per magazine.

Recognizing the potential, several private carriers have now established new companies specifically geared to this combination of private delivery. The delivery of unaddressed circulars is essential to this concept, a service that cannot be matched by the U.S. Postal Service.

But now the post office is trying to make magazines captive customers. A proposed regulation of the Postal Service would, in effect, define a circular bearing no name and address as ''addressed'' when delivered with a publication. This predatory action would greatly reduce business agreements between magazine publishers and private distributors since the benefits to both parties (increased profits to carriers and reduced costs to publishers) would be eliminated. It is lu-

102

103

dicrous to interpret an unaddressed circular as an addressed letter.

The proposed regulation would have a disastrous effect on the printing firms of America. About 20 billion circulars per year are printed and distributed with newspapers in the same way that private carriers are distributing identical circulars with magazines. The Postal Service's proposal, enlarging the scope of its monopoly power, might well jeopardize the printing of the 20 billion circulars. Many of the advertisers sending out these circulars could not afford the much more costly distribution through the mail. So a large portion of them would never be distributed and probably never be printed, and the printing industry and the consumers would take another fleecing from big government.

Government Employee Training Programs. The U.S. Civil Service Commission maintains regional training centers in cities throughout the country. These training centers provide instruction for federal civil servants available from local private-sector learning centers. For example, the Reading Skills Institute, Inc., in Des Moines, Iowa, provides reading improvement instruction for the general public, businesses, professional organizations, and similar groups. The institute's executive training program emphasizes skills required for business and professional reading. A large segment of the firm's potential market is government workers located in Iowa. Approximately 16 percent of the total work force in the Des Moines metropolitan area, or 28,500 persons, is employed by federal, state, and local governments. Many of these people are encouraged to take reading improvement courses to better their job performance.

Instead of sending employees to local centers like the Reading Skills Institute, the federal government makes its workers attend the St. Louis Regional Training Center where the Civil Service Commission offers a program entitled "Accelerated Reading." The travel expenses involved in sending a government employee from Des Moines to a training session in St. Louis are high. Just the round-trip air fare plus a conservative daily allowance for room and board for four days exceeds the tuition charged by Reading Skills Institute for classes con ducted anywhere within the state of Iowa. Additional costs would include employee time away from job, cost of instruction at the training center, miscellaneous travel expenses such as transportation between the airport, the training center, and the hotel, and program development costs.

The federal program is not only expensive, but ineffective. According to the course description, an employee will be able to increase reading efficiency by 50 percent. Therefore, an employee reading 10 hours per week who is paid $10 per hour would save $25 per week. At that rate, it would take at least 11 weeks to recover just the travel costs. Testimony by a representative of the Reading Skills Institute indicated that the average graduate of its program increased his reading efficiency by between 100 and 200 percent. By requiring employees to attend government training programs, bureaucrats are able to kill two birds with one stone: they acquire additional functions and programs, and make it almost impossible for private firms to compete.

Government In-House Pest-Control Service. Many federal installations such as office buildings, veterans hospitals, research facilities, schools, etc., contract with private firms for pest-control service. A major exception is the Department of Defense. Although DOD activities are covered by Circular A-76, the agency has managed to avoid contracting out for pest control. Testimony by a DOD entomologist before the Small Business Administration pointed out that when staff reductions and private-sector contracting were suggested for less expensive and higher-quality pest control, agency staff personnel undertook predatory activity. To stop sending cost and productivity reports to the Office of Management and Budget, correspondence from DOD to OMB concerning pest control was censored so that references to staff reductions were eliminated. The expert at DOD who favored contracting out for pest-control service was harassed constantly. When he threatened to go to his congressman to complain about efforts to block his reports, attempts were made to discredit him. He was unjustly accused of defrauding the government of educational support money, which he obtained to attend graduate school. Also, his appearance at committee meetings was carefully controlled and he was instructed not to mention his suggestions for improving pest-control services.

At the SBA hearings in Des Moines, it was pointed out that contracting out for pest-control services was strongly resisted by a large bureaucracy of unnecessary support services that had developed around DOD's pest-control system consisting of (1) in-house pest-control personnel training and certification (all commercial firms are required to be certified and employ trained personnel); (2) in-house pesticide supply systems; and (3) in-house administrative staff. Therefore, greedy bureaucrats once again cost taxpayers millions of dollars by doing what could be done more economically by private firms.

Energy Conservation. The most rapid expansion of government bureaucracy in recent years has probably taken place in the field of energy. Because of what is deemed a pressing need for energy conservation, federal, state, and even local governments have succeeded in developing programs said to improve the efficiency of energy consumption. One such program was the construction and operation of a pilot fiber insulation plant by the state of Iowa (with considerable federal grant help) called Mid-Sioux Opportunity, Inc. The plant's function was to act as an experimental model, and to provide insulation for the homes of poor, handicapped, and low-income people. However, for reasons that are obvious by now, the plant expanded its operation to include general insulation sales.

Cellulose fiber insulation sales by the state of Iowa and other states have devastated much of the private cellulose wood fiber manufacturing industry. Testimony given by the president of a private manufacturing firm, Iowa Excel Corporation, at the SBA hearings in Des Moines, revealed that in 1975 Iowa Excel Corporation was a growing firm with annual sales of $318,531. By 1977 sales had climbed to almost a million dollars, nearly a 200 percent increase. The company had become so successful that it invested in an additional plant and got an SBA-guaranteed loan. Then, in 1978, the Iowa state government entered into the insulation business charging below-market prices. Within one year Iowa Excel's sales dropped to $150,000. The very next year, 1979, Iowa Excel went bankrupt and was forced to default on its SBA loan! When a number of commercial insulation manufacturing firms asked why the Iowa state government decided to start competing with the private sector, they were told that agency studies showed a shortage in cellulose wood fiber insulation. So, in order to make enough available, the state had to produce it. However, the president of Iowa Excel wrote letters to all state agencies not only in Iowa, but also in Minnesota, Wisconsin, Illinois, and others. He asked about seasonal demands for fiber insulation and indicated that the company would be happy to keep its plant in operation during slack months in order to supply insulation to the state government. There were never any responses to these letters.

Another energy case involved DSET Labs, Inc., of Phoenix, Arizona. DSET was a highly successful firm that performed precision testing of solar collectors. The firm's testing services were regarded as among the best in the country, and solar panel manufacturers greatly valued an approval by DSET. Much of DSET's business came from sun-belt states such as Florida. Things were going well with the firm until the government created the energy crisis and started some conservation programs at state universities. Solar energy research and testing centers were developed and expanded at federal- and state-supported colleges and universities all over the country. Soon these centers were competing with private firms in virtually every aspect of solar energy production, including precision testing. The state of Florida established a solar energy institute financed by both the federal and the state government. One of its primary functions was the precision testing of solar collectors. To make sure that the institute's testing service would not have to compete with private firms, the state imposed a regulation that required all solar collectors marketed in Florida to be tested and certified by the solar energy institute.

Almost overnight, DSET Labs lost its Florida market. In addition, SBA testimony showed that the quality of the testing service deteriorated under state control. It was pointed out that private testing firms like DSET Labs maintained a high level of quality control because it faced the likelihood of legal action if a solar collector failed to perform. However, the state organizations had very little quality control because no one could be held accountable if a solar collector went blooey. It is almost impossible to sue the state for poor performance.

Child Day-Care Centers. Testimony before the Small Business Administration shows that state and local government agencies have aggressively used federal assistance to establish child day-care centers. Nonprofit organizations have also used government subsidies to provide child day-care services. It was demonstrated that when government subsidies are taken into account, the cost of publicly supported child day care is at least twice as much as comparable private day care. Yet, government at all levels continues to plump for publicly supported child care in order to feather the nests of the bureaucrats that supervise the services. The often-used argument in favor of public child day care is that disadvantaged children will be excluded because their parents can't pay for private service. However, as pointed out earlier, the government could help disadvantaged families by giving them vouchers to present at the day-care center of their choice, or, better yet, tax credits.

We have outlined only a handful of cases involving unfair government competition with private business. There are thousands of them. The Small Business Administration lists nearly one hundred industries in which government competes with small private firms.[8] Over 50 business representatives testified in two hearings conducted by the SBA in Des Moines, and in Washington, D.C. In many cases, testimony was provided by trade association staff members in behalf of hundreds of thousands of individual private businessmen. The harm done to the economy and the taxpayer through unfair and unnecessary competition from the government is incalculable.

NOTES TO CHAPTER 6

[1]See Small Business Administration, *Government Competition: A Threat to Small Business* (Washington, D.C.: Office of the Chief Council for Advocacy, 1980), p. 105; and Bennett and Johnson, *The Political Economy of Federal Government Growth,* p. 21

[2]Small Business Administration, *Government Competition,* p. vii.

[3]*Ibid.,* p. 48.

[4]U.S. General Accounting Office, *Development of a National Make-or-Buy Strategy—Process and Problems PSAD-78-18* (Washington, D.C.: Comptroller General of the United States, September 25, 1978).

[5]Barbara Blumenthal, "Uncle Sam's Army of Invisible Employees," *National Journal* (May 5, 1977) p. 732.

[6]Small Business Administration, *Government Competition,* p. 112.

[7]*Ibid.,* p. 68.

[8]*Ibid.,* pp. 147–69.

7

CONCLUSION

Our conclusion is inescapable. All of the evidence, without exception, proves that the people of the United States can have better government—federal, state, and local—at much lower cost by contracting out the production of goods and services to private firms by competitive bidding.

Taxes can be cut dramatically, yet no government services need to be reduced (though perhaps many should be). The faith of the people in their government can be restored only when waste, inefficiency, empire building, and outright theft are eliminated from the public sector. The facts we have presented show that this can be done by applying the Bureaucratic Rule of Two.

Of course, the goal we set will be difficult to reach. The public service unions, the bureaucratic profiteers, and the complacent politicians who reap personal benefits from the present system will fight to the last against a loss of power, jobs, perquisites, and graft.

Unless, however, the cost of government is drastically reduced, the bloat of government shrunk, and trust in government restored, the United States is certain to slip further and further into an economic and social morass that can destroy us as a world power.

We have already seen the proliferation of tax revolts throughout the land. We have already seen vast tax evasion by workers who believe that their income taken in taxes is being poured down a rathole. This trend will continue to sow the seeds of social unrest, lawlessness, and universal disgust with government. The proposal we make can help reverse those trends. Perhaps the best way to start on this new road to better government would be to pass a constitutional amendment prohibiting Congress from spending more than it receives in taxes. By taking away from Congress the power to keep spending more and more without limit, a brake on government profligacy could be applied.[1]

Liberals who wish to keep the expensive social welfare programs now in place may find that contracting out services to private firms will make it possible not only to continue, but to improve these programs. Conservatives who are demanding that the costs of government be drastically reduced can achieve their goals by applying the Bureaucratic Rule of Two. The average American worker and taxpayer could be led to give his wholehearted support to politicians who take up this challenge to reform and restore the American way of life.

People of all political and social beliefs can have renewed hope that by forcing the bureaucrats to serve the public instead of themselves, a stronger and better America can be built.

NOTES TO CHAPTER 7

[1]The mechanics of the reduction in taxation at the local government level have been discussed in detail in Robert W. Poole's excellent book *Cutting Back City Hall* (New York: Universe Books, 1979). Another outstanding book dealing with every aspect of private-sector production of local services has been edited by Mark Frazier and Walter Olson for the Taxpayers' Foundation in Washington, D.C. This second work, *More for Less: Tax-Saving Reforms in Local Services,* includes the chapter "How to Introduce Tax-Saving Attitudes." Both books provide excellent insights for the concerned citizen.

AUTHOR INDEX

SUBJECT INDEX

114

An Important Book That Deserves
Wide Distribution to Local,
State & National Political Leaders

BETTER GOVERNMENT
AT HALF THE PRICE

you can begin the task of cutting the
cost of your government right now, by
distributing copies of this book. Bulk
copy orders receive generous discounts
and are shipped the day they are received,
postpaid by the publisher. Order now
*"Carefully developed and tightly reasoned.
The authors show how taxes can be reduced
without cutting public services."* — *William E. Simon,
Author, A TIME FOR TRUTH.*

QUANTITY PRICES

1 copy	$ 5.95	10 copies	$ 35.00	100 copies	$ 200.00
3 copies	$15.00	25 copies	$ 80.00	500 copies	$ 650.00
5 copies	$20.00	50 copies	$150.00	1000 copies	$1000.00